Yucatán Peninsula

Richard Arghiris & Anna Maria Espsäter

Credits

Footprint credits
Editor: Felicity Laughton
Production and layout: Emma Bryers
Maps: Kevin Feeney

Managing Director: Andy Riddle
Commercial Director: Patrick Dawson
Publisher: Alan Murphy
Publishing Managers: Felicity Laughton,
Nicola Gibbs
Digital Editors: Jo Williams, Tom Mellors
Marketing and PR: Liz Harper
Sales: Diane McEntee
Advertising: Renu Sibal
Finance and Administration: Elizabeth
Taylor

Photography credits
Front cover: Andrew Howard / Shutterstock
Back cover: K Kulikov / Shutterstock

Printed in Great Britain by CPI Antony Rowe,
Chippenham, Wiltshire

MIX
Paper from
responsible sources
FSC
www.fsc.org
FSC® C013604

Every effort has been made to ensure that
the facts in this guidebook are accurate.
However, travellers should still obtain advice
from consulates, airlines, etc, about travel
and visa requirements before travelling.
The authors and publishers cannot accept
responsibility for any loss, injury or
inconvenience however caused.

Publishing information
Footprint *Focus Yucatán Peninsula*
1st edition
© Footprint Handbooks Ltd
September 2011

ISBN: 978 1 908206 24 4
CIP DATA: A catalogue record for this book
is available from the British Library

® Footprint Handbooks and the Footprint
mark are a registered trademark of Footprint
Handbooks Ltd

Published by Footprint
6 Riverside Court
Lower Bristol Road
Bath BA2 3DZ, UK
T +44 (0)1225 469141
F +44 (0)1225 469461
footprinttravelguides.com

Distributed in the USA by Globe Pequot Press,
Guilford, Connecticut

The content of Footprint *Focus Yucatán
Peninsula* has been taken directly from
Footprint's *Central America Handbook* which
was researched and written by Richard
Arghiris and Peter Hutchison.

Contents

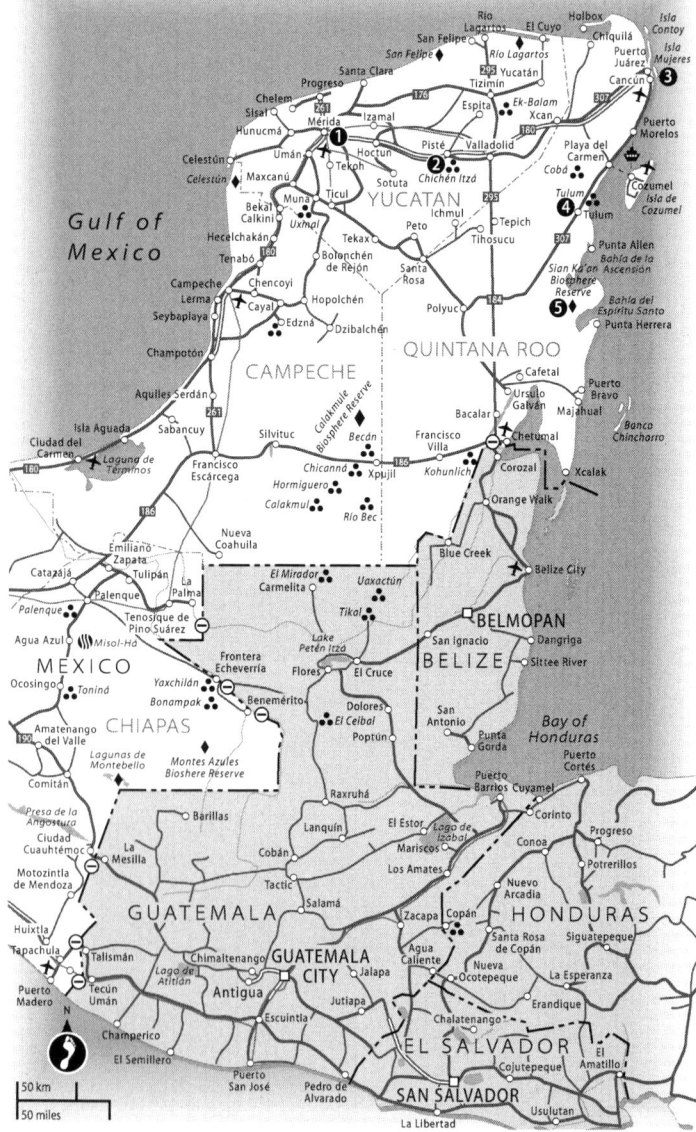

Holbox
Isla
Contoy
Río
Lagartos
El Cuyo
Chiquilá
Isla
Mujeres
San Felipe
Río Lagartos
Puerto
Juárez
3
Santa Clara
San Felipe
Yucatán
Cancún
Progreso
Tizimín
Chelem
180
Sisal
Espita
Ek-Balam
Xcan
Puerto
Morelos
Hunucmá
Mérida
Izamal
1
Celestún
Hoctún
Pisté
Valladolid
Playa del
Carmen
Umán
Tekoh
Cobá
Cozumel
Maxcanú
Sotuta
2
Chichén Itzá
Isla de
Cozumel
Celestún
Muna
Ticul
YUCATAN
Bekal
Calkiní
Uxmal
Tulum
4
Tulum
Hecelchakán
Tekax
Peto
Ichmul
Tepich
Punta Allen
Bahía de la
Ascensión
Tenabó
Bolonchén
de Rejón
Santa
Rosa
Tihosuco
Sian Ka'an
Biosphere
Reserve
Campeche
Chencoyi
Hopolchén
5
Bahía del
Espíritu Santo
Punta Herrera
Lerma
Cayal
Seybaplaya
Edzná
Dzibalchén
Polyuc
Champotón
CAMPECHE
QUINTANA ROO
Cafetal
Aquiles Serdán
Úrsulo
Galván
Puerto
Bravo
Sabancuy
Silvituc
Calakmul
Biosphere Reserve
Majahual
Isla Aguada
Bacalar
Ciudad del
Carmen
Laguna de
Términos
Becán
Francisco
Villa
Chetumal
Banco
Chinchorro
Francisco
Escárcega
Chicanná
Xpujil
186
Kohunlich
Corozal
Xcalak
Hormiguero
Calakmul
Río Bec
Orange Walk
186
Nueva
Coahuila
Blue Creek
Emiliano
Zapata
Tulipán
El Mirador
Carmelita
Uaxactún
Belize City
Catazajá
La
Palma
Palenque
Tikal
BELMOPAN
Palenque
Tenosique de
Pino Suárez
Lake
Petén Itzá
San Ignacio
Dangriga
Agua Azul
Misol-Ha
Frontera
Echeverría
Flores
El Cruce
BELIZE
Sittee River
MEXICO
Ocosingo
Toniná
Yaxchilán
Bonampak
Benemérito
Dolores
El Ceibal
Poptún
San
Antonio
Bay of
Honduras
Amatenango
del Valle
CHIAPAS
Punta
Gorda
Puerto
Cortés
Comitán
Lagunas
de Montebello
Montes Azules
Biosphere Reserve
Raxruhá
Puerto
Barrios
Cuyamel
Presa de
la Angostura
Barillas
Lanquín
El Estor
Lago de
Izabal
Corinto
Progreso
Ciudad
Cuauhtémoc
Cobán
Mariscos
Conoa
Potrerillos
Motozintla
de Mendoza
La
Mesilla
Tactic
Los Amates
Nuevo
Arcadia
Huixtla
Salamá
Zacapa
Copán
HONDURAS
GUATEMALA
Santa Rosa
de Copán
Siguatepeque
Tapachula
Talismán
Chimaltenango
GUATEMALA
CITY
Jalapa
Agua
Caliente
Nueva
Ocotepeque
La Esperanza
Tecún
Umán
Lago de
Atitlán
Antigua
Jutiapa
Chalatenango
Erandique
Puerto
Madero
Champerico
Escuintla
EL SALVADOR
El
Amatillo
El Semillero
Puerto
San José
Pedro de
Alvarado
Cojutepeque
SAN SALVADOR
Usulután
N
La Libertad

Gulf of
Mexico

50 km
50 miles

The Yucatán Peninsula, which includes the states of Campeche, Yucatán and Quintana Roo, is sold to tourists as the land of Maya archaeology and Caribbean beach resorts. And there's no denying it, the warm turquoise sea, fringed with fine white-sand beaches and palm groves of the 'Mayan Riviera' are second to none. And it would be a crime not to tread the beaten path to the sensational ruins at Chichén Itzá, Uxmal and Tulum. But it more than pays to explore beyond the main itineraries to visit some of the lesser-known Maya sites such as Cobá, Edzná or Dzibilchaltún, or the imposing Franciscan monastery and huge pyramid at Izamal. There are flamingo feeding grounds at Celestún and Río Lagartos and over 500 other species of bird, many of which are protected in Sian Ka'an Biosphere Reserve, which covers 4500 sq km of tropical forest, savannah, and coastline. Ever since Jacques Cousteau filmed the Palancar Reef in the 1960s, divers have swarmed to the clear waters of Cozumel, the 'Island of the Swallows', to wonder at the many species of coral and other underwater plants and creatures, at what has become one of the most popular diving centres in the world. Also popular and specialized is diving in the many *cenotes* (sink holes), including the famous Nohooch Nah Chich, part of the world's largest underground cave system.

Planning your trip

Where to go

Composed of three neighbouring states – Campeche, Yucatán and Quintana Roo – the Yucatán Peninsula is full of ruins from Mayan history. The Puuc civilization reached its zenith at the regal city of Uxmal, whilst sprawling Chichén Itzá is famous for its shadow serpents which appear twice a year at the passing of the equinoxes. The Yucatán's beaches are as legendary as its archaeological sites and, if you like to party, you'll love Cancún, an American-style resort perched on Caribbean shores. If you're looking for something a little quieter, a short journey will take you to the beaches of Isla Mujeres or Tulum, where you can snorkel and dive, or simply relax in soothing waters. Equally, if you're seeking urban refinement, Mérida – the capital of Yucatán state and the so-called 'White City' – is steeped in history and grand colonial architecture.

Suggested itinerary
Heading in a clockwise arc around the Yucatán Peninsula, stop off in the colonial town of Campeche before making base at Mérida. Nearby, Chichén Itzá is an obligatory stop, also accessible from the nearby colonial town of Valladolid, but if you keep heading east you'll eventually land in Cancún. From here it's easy to jump between beaches and ruins en route south to the Belize border – Tulum and Coba are particularly recommended. After following the Ruta Maya through Belize, Honduras and Guatemala, you can loop back into Mexico at Frontera Echeverría, easily accessible from Tikal.

When to go

The best time to visit southern Mexico is from October to April when there is virtually no rain, although the mountains can be quite chilly, especially December to February. Rainy seasons lasts May to October, which is also hurricane season in the Caribbean. Don't be put off by the term 'rainy season' – most years, the rains only affect travellers for an hour or two a day. August is holiday time for Mexicans and this can make accommodation scarce in the smaller resorts. Semana Santa (Easter week), the Christmas holidays, Day of the Dead celebrations (at the beginning of November) and other important local fiestas are also busy times; book ahead. ▸▸ *For festival dates, see page 14.*

What to do

Southern Mexico's coastline of reefs and lagoons, and its expanse of mountains cut by long rivers and protected areas make it extremely well suited to many types of outdoor adventure. The **Asociación Mexicana de Turismo de Aventura y Ecoturismo (AMTAVE)** ① *Félix Cuevas 224-b, Col del Valle, CP 03100, México DF, T/F55-5575 7887, www.amtave.org,* is making steady progress in promoting and protecting ecotourism nationwidealongside adventure-related pursuits. The need for standards is important in some activities and **AMTAVE** is doing plenty to develop awareness in this field.

Don't miss ...

Numbers relate to map on page 4.

Caving

Caving, or speleology, in Mexico is more than just going down into deep dark holes. Sometimes it is a sport more closely related to canyoning as there are some excellent underground river scrambles. The biggest cave systems in the country are in Chiapas, especially around Tuxtla Gutiérrez, but you also have the option of diving in water-filled caves known as *cenotes*, a common and popular sport in the Yucatán, particularly around **Tulum**.

Diving

Quintana Roo offers warm-water reefs close to the shore and visibility of over 30 m. **Cozumel** has some of the best diving in the world. There are marine parks at Chankanaab and at Palancar Reef with numerous caves and gullies and a horseshoe-shaped diving arena. Also excellent on the west side of the island are Santa Rosa and sites off San Francisco beach. To the southwest are good sites off Laguna Colombia, while off Punta Sur there is excellent deep diving. There is concern, however, over the damage to the reef inflicted by the cruise ship pier, and more of these piers are planned. At **Isla Mujeres**, also in Quintana Roo, the most-dived sites include Los Manchones, La Bandera, a shallow dive south of the island, and El Frío, a deep wreck 1½ hrs to the north.

Trekking

It's possible to trek between ruins and *cenotes* (sink holes) in the tropical forests of the Yucatán Peninsula, but during the dry season they offer little shade and can be extremely hot. For more on trekking, see National parks, below.

National parks

Mexico has an immense range of habitats and wildlife – the far south is in the Neotropical kingdom, home to a wealth of tropical forest species. National parks in Mexico were set up a long time ago primarily to provide green recreation areas for city dwellers; they are generally small and have often been planted with imported species such as eucalyptus, and are thus of no biological value. However, the country does also have a good number of biosphere reserves, which are both of great biological value and suitable for tourism.

In the Yucatán Peninsula the **Sian Ka'an Biosphere Reserve**, south of Cancún, is a mixture of forest, savannah and mangrove swamp, best visited on a day-trip run by **Amigos de Sian Ka'an** ① *Calle Fuego 2 SM, Cancún, T998-892 2958, www.amigosdesian kaan.org*. Also useful is the **Sian Ka'an Information Centre** ① *Av Tulum between Satelite and Geminis, Tulum, T/F984-871 2363, siankaan_tours@hotmail.com*. It is also well worth visiting the **Río Lagartos** and **Río Celestún** reserves on the north and west coasts of Yucatán, well known for their flamingos. The **Calakmul Biosphere Reserve** is important mainly for its Mayan ruins, seeming to the layman more like scrub than forest.

Information on national parks and biosphere reserves can be obtained from the **Instituto Nacional de Ecología** ① *Periférico 5000, Col Insurgentes Cuicuilco, CP 04530, Delegación Coyoacán, México DF, T55-5424 6400, www.ine.gob.mx.*

Getting there

Air
Airport information There are several international airports in Mexico, the two busiest are **Mexico City** and **Cancún**. If you are likely to be returning home at a busy time (eg between Christmas and New Year, or August) a booking is advisable on open-return tickets. When arriving in Mexico by air, make sure you fill in the immigration document before joining the queue to have your passport checked.

Departure tax Currently US$40 on international flights (dollars or pesos accepted); always check when purchasing if departure tax is included in ticket price. A sales tax of 15% is payable on domestic plane tickets bought in Mexico.

Student/youth and discount fares Some airlines are flexible on the age limit, others strict. One way and returns available, or 'Open Jaws' (flying into one point and returning from another). Do not assume student tickets are the cheapest, though they are often very flexible.

From Europe To Mexico City: there are several airlines that have regular direct flights. From Amsterdam with **KLM**; from Frankfurt with **Lufthansa** and **AeroMéxico** (LTU and Condor charter flights to Mexico City or Cancún); from London and Manchester with **British Airways**; from Barcelona with **Iberia**; from Madrid with **Iberia** and **AeroMéxico**; from Paris with **Air France** and **AeroMéxico**. Most connecting flights in Europe are through Madrid or Gatwick. Fares vary from airline to airline and according to time of year. Check with an agency for the best deal for when you wish to travel. **To Cancún**: from Amsterdam with **Martinair**; Dusseldorf with LTU; Frankfurt with LTU and **Condor**; Munich with LTU and **Condor**; Madrid with **AeroMéxico** and **Avianca**; Milan with **Lauda Air**; and Paris with **American Airlines**.

From USA To Mexico City: a large number of airlines fly this route, including **American Airlines**, AeroMéxico, Delta, Continental, United, Northwest, Taesa and **Americawest**. Flights are available from most major cities, with the cheapest generally going through Miami, Dallas, Houston and sometimes Los Angeles. **To Cancún**: Flights leave from many cities across the USA.

From Canada To Mexico City: the options are less varied, but there are direct flights from Montreal and Toronto, as well as regular flights from other main cities. From Toronto with **United**; and from Vancouver with **Japan Airlines**. Keep an eye out for special offers, which can be extremely good value (often at very short notice).

From Australia and New Zealand From Sydney with United and from Auckland with Air New Zealand, all flying through Los Angeles.

From Latin America and the Caribbean Flights from Latin America have increased in recent years. Central America is covered by the TACA network, connecting the capitals of each country to Mexico City and some of the smaller regional cities. In South America, connections are to capitals and major cities. If planning a trip to Cuba there are flights from Cancún, Mérida and Mexico City with Cubana.

Road
From USA There are many border crossings with the US; the main ones are Tijuana, Mexicali, Nogales, Ciudad Juárez, Piedras Negras, Nuevo Laredo and Matamoros.

From Guatemala The main border town is Tapachula, with a crossing over the Talismán Bridge or at Ciudad Hidalgo. A more interesting route is via Ciudad Cuauhtémoc or heading northwest from Santa Elena/Flores towards Tenosique. There are also options for road and river travel.

From Belize The border crossing at Santa Elena is near Chetumal, where public transport can be arranged. A very quiet – and more challenging – crossing is at Blue Creek.

Getting around

Air
Most medium-sized towns in Mexico have an airport. If you're looking to cover a great distance in a short time, several airlines fly internal routes (a few with international flights as well) including Aeromar, Aeroméxico Connect, Taesa, and Aviacsa. Low-cost airlines include: Interjet (www.interjet.com.mx), Volaris (www.volaris.com.mx) and VivaAerobus (www.vivaaerobus.com). General costs are comparable with the older airlines – you get the bargain if you can book ahead, travel at inconvenient times or if there is a special offer.

Bus → *Buses are often called camiones, hence 'Central Camionero' for bus station.*
The Mexican bus system is very extensive and efficient. In some cities there is a central bus terminal (in Mexico City there are four – one at each point of the compass), in others there are a couple – one for first-class services, one for second. A third variation is division by companies. The entire network is privatized and highly competitive, although in practise there is often little difference between carriers. Most inter-city routes are served by comfortable and very adequate first-class buses with reclining seats, air conditioning, Spanish-language movies and on-board toilet. For those seeking extra luxury, several companies offer superior class services, so-called Primera Plus or Ejecutiva, which include a soft-drink, snack and almost horizontally aligned seats. It is highly advisable to book your tickets several days in advance when travelling at Christmas, Semana Santa or other national holidays. If your journey is longer than six hours, it is sensible to book 24 hours ahead. If travelling overnight, pack a sweater or blanket in your hand-luggage – the air-conditioning gets icy. Also avoid sitting near the toilet (it invariably smells) and bring snacks and water.

Fares Bus travel can use up a lot of your budget because the distances covered are great. As a very rough calculation, bus travel works out at around US$5 per hour spent travelling.

First-class fares are usually 10% dearer than second-class ones and the superior classes 30-40% more than first-class. On a long journey you can save the price of a hotel room by travelling overnight, but in some areas this is dangerous and not recommended.

Useful bus links

Some bus tickets can be purchased at www.ticketbus.com.mx, information on T01-800-702-8000.
ADO GL, www.adogl.com.mx, T01-800-702-8000. The Yucatán, southeast, Gulf and northeast Mexico.

Cristóbal Colón, T01-800-702-8000. South of Mexico City. Details on the Ticketbus system.
ETN, www.etn.com.mx, T01-800-8000-386.
Grupo Estrella, www.estrellablanca.com.mx, T01-800-507-5500. Most of Mexico through several companies.
Primera Plus, www.primeraplus.com.mx, T01-800-375-7587. Mid-central to southern Mexico.

Bicycle

The Yucatán Peninsula offers plenty of enjoyable places for cycling. The main problems facing cyclists are heavy traffic, poor road conditions and a lack of specialized spare parts, particularly for mountain bikes, which can only be found in big cities. The easiest region for cycling is the Gulf of Mexico coast, but many of the roads are flat and boring. The toll roads are generally preferable to the ordinary highways for cyclists; there is less traffic, more lanes and a wide paved shoulder, but take lots of water as there are few facilities. **Tip**: if you walk your bicycle on the pavement through the toll station you don't have to pay. Cycling on some main roads can be very dangerous; fit a rear-view mirror.

Car hire

Car rental is very expensive in Mexico, from US$35-45 a day for a basic model (plus15% sales tax). The age limit is normally at least 25 and you'll need to place a deposit, normally against a credit card, for damage. It can be cheaper to arrange hire in the US or Europe. At some tourist resorts, however, such as Cancún, you can pick up a VW Beetle convertible for US$25 per day. Renting a vehicle is nearly impossible without a credit card. It is twice as expensive to leave a car at a different point from the starting point than it is to make a round trip. Rates will vary from city to city. Make sure you have unlimited mileage.

Assistance Angeles Verdes (Green Angels) patrol many of Mexico's main roads. Call them toll-free on T01-800-903-9200; every state also has an Angeles Verdes hotline. The drivers speak English, are trained to give first aid, make minor auto repairs and deal with flat tyres. Assistance is provided free of charge, you pay for the gas.

Petrol/diesel All *gasolina* is now unleaded and all petrol stations are franchised by Petróleos Mexicanos (PEMEX). Fuel costs the same throughout the country (approximately US$0.65 a litre). Diesel is also available. Petrol stations are not self-service; it is normal to give the attendant a small tip.

Road tolls A toll is called a *cuota*, as opposed to a non-toll road, which is a *vía libre*. There are many toll charges and the cost works out at around one peso per kilometre. Check out your route, and toll prices, on the **Traza Tu Ruta** section of www.sct.gob.mx.

Warnings On all roads, if the driver flashes his lights he is claiming right of way and the oncoming traffic must give way. At *Alto* (Halt) signs, all traffic must come to a complete stop. Always avoid driving at night – night-time robberies are on the increase. 'Sleeping policemen' or road bumps can be hazardous as there are often no warning signs; they are sometimes marked *zona de topes*, or incorrectly marked as *vibradores*.

Hitchhiking
Hitchhiking in Mexico is not recommended as it is not universally safe (seek local advice). It is very easy to hitch short distances, such as the last few kilometres to an archaeological site off the main road; offer to pay something, like US$0.50.

Motorcycle
Motorcycling is good in southern Mexico as most main roads are in fairly good condition and hotels are usually willing to allow the bike to be parked in a courtyard or patio. In the major tourist centres, such as Playa del Carmen or Cancún, motorbike parts can be found as there are Honda dealers for bike and jet-ski rentals.

Taxi
To avoid overcharging, the government has taken control of taxi services from airports to cities. Only those with government licences are allowed to carry passengers from the airport and you can usually buy a ticket with a set price to your destination from a booth at the terminal. Tipping is not required unless the driver helps with heavy luggage or provides some extra service.

Maps
Guía Roji publish a wide range of regional maps, city plans and gazettes, available at most bookshops and news-stands. Guia Roji is online at http://guiaroji.com.mx with full street, town, city and state search facilities for the country.

Sleeping

Hotels and hospedajes
The cheapest places to stay are *casas de huéspedes*, but these are often very basic and dirty. Budget hotels are a gamble that sometimes pays off; always check amenities and room before accepting. The middle categories are still reasonable value by US and European standards, but high-end hotels have become increasingly expensive as tourism has flourished. Motels and auto-hotels are usually hourly rental, but can make clean and acceptable overnight lodgings for weary drivers.

There is a hotel tax, ranging between 1% and 4%, according to the state. Check-out time is commonly 1100 but bag storage is commonplace. Rooms are normally charged at a flat rate, or if there are single rooms they are around 80% the price of a double, so sharing works out cheaper. A room with a double bed is usually cheaper than one with two singles. A room with three or more sharing is often very economical, even in the mid-price range. Beware of 'helpers' who try to find you a hotel, as prices quoted at the hotel desk rise to give them commission. During peak season (November to April) it may be hard to find a room. The week after Easter is normally a holiday, so prices remain high. Discounts on hotel prices can often be arranged in the low season (May to October), but this is more difficult in the Yucatán.

Youth hostels
Hostels are very much on the increase and many of them are excellent. They are not always great value for couples, however – a shared hotel room is often more comfortable and economical. Both private and International Youth Hostel endorsed accommodation are widely available; the latter offers discounts for members. For more information contact **Hostelling International Mexico** ① *Guatemala 4, Col Centro, Mexico City, T55-5518 1726, www.hostellingmexico.com*. Additionally, many towns have a **Villa Deportiva Juvenil**, the Mexican equivalent of a youth hostel, sometimes basic and normally very cheap.

Camping
Most sites are called 'trailer parks', but tents are usually allowed. However, due to their primary role as trailer parks they're often in locations more suited for people with their own transport than people on public transport. **Playas Públicas**, with a blue and white sign of a palm tree, are beaches where camping is allowed. They are usually cheap, sometimes free and some have shelters and basic amenities. You can often camp in or near national parks, although you must speak first with the guards, and usually pay a small fee.

Sleeping and eating price codes

Sleeping

$$$$	over US$150	**$$$**	US$66-150
$$	US$30-65	**$**	under US$30

Price codes refer to a standard double/twin room in high season.

Eating

$$$	over US$15	**$$**	US$8-15	**$**	under US$8

Price codes refer to the cost of a two-course meal, not including drinks.

Eating and drinking

Food

Food for most Mexicans represents an integral part of their national identity and much has been written since the 1960s about the evolution of Mexican cooking. Experts suggest that there have been three important developmental stages: first, the combination of the indigenous and the Spanish traditions; later, the influence of other European cuisines, notably the French in the 19th century; and finally the adoption of exotic oriental dishes and fast food from the USA in the 20th century. In 2010, the importance of Mexican food was recognized by its inclusion on the UNESCO Intangible Cultural Heritage List.

Mexican cuisine is usually perceived as spicy or hot due to the prolific use of chilli peppers, but equally, maize is a very typical ingredient and has been a staple crop since ancient times. It is mainly consumed in *antojitos* (snacks) and some of the most common are tacos, *quesadillas, flautas, sopes, tostadas, tlacoyos* and *gorditas*, which consist of various shapes and sizes of *tortillas*, with a variety of fillings and usually garnished with a hot sauce.

Meals in Mexico consist of breakfast, a heavy lunch between 1400 and 1500 and a light supper between 1800 and 2000. Costs in modest establishments are US$2-3 for breakfast, US$2.50-3.50 for set lunch (US$4-6 for a special *comida corrida*) and US$5-10 for dinner (generally no set menu). A la carte meals at modest establishments cost about US$8-12. A very good meal can be had for US$15 at a middle-level establishment. Street stalls are by far the cheapest – although not always the safest – option. The best value is undoubtedly in small, family-run places. If self-catering, markets are cheaper than supermarkets.

Drink

There are always plenty of non-alcoholic *refrescos* (soft drinks) and mineral water. *Agua fresca* – fresh fruit juices mixed with water or mineral water – and *licuados* (milk shakes) are good and usually safe. Herbal teas, for example chamomile (*manzanilla*) and mint (*hierba buena*), are readily available.

The native alcoholic drinks are **pulque**, made from the fermented juice of the agave plant, **tequila** and **mezcal**, both made from distilled agave. Mezcal usually has a *gusano de maguey* (worm) in the bottle, considered to be a particular delicacy but, contrary to popular myth, is not hallucinogenic. National **beer** is also good with a wide range of light and dark varieties.

Festivals and events

If any of these holidays falls on a Thursday or a Tuesday, they are usually an excuse for a *puente*, a long weekend (which can have implications for travel, hotel accommodation and services).

National holidays
I Jan New Year
5 Feb Constitution Day
21 Mar Birthday of Benito Juárez
Mar/Apr Maundy Thu, Good Fri, Easter Sat
1 May Labour Day
5 May Battle of Puebla
1 Sep El Informe (Presidential Message)
16 Sep Independence Day
12 Oct Día de la Raza (Discovery of America)

20 Nov Día de la Revolución (Revolution Day)
25 Dec Christmas Day

Religious fiestas
There are more than 5000 religious festivals each year. The most widely celebrated are:
6 Jan Santos Reyes (Three Kings)
10 May Día de las Madres (Mothers' Day)
1-2 Nov Día de los Muertos (All Souls' Day)
12 Dec La Virgen de Guadalupe

Shopping

The colourful markets and craft shops are a highlight of any visit to the Yucatán Peninsula. The *artesanía* is an amalgam of ancient and modern designs influenced mainly by the traditional popular art forms of local indigenous communities. Colonial towns such as Mérida are convenient market centres for seeing the superb range of products from functional pots to scary masks hanging over delicately embroidered robes and gleaming lacquered chests.

Weaving and textile design go back a long way and the variety on offer is huge. They can be spun in cotton or wool on the traditional *telar de cintura*, a 'waist loom', or *telar de pie*, a pedal-operated loom introduced by the Spanish. Many woven items are on sale in the markets, from *sarapes* and *morrales* (shoulder bags) to wall-hangings, rugs and bedspreads. Synthetic fibres are often used, so make sure you know what you're getting.

Essentials A-Z

Customs and duty free

The list of permitted items is extensive and generally allows for anything that could reasonably be considered for personal use. Adults entering Mexico are allowed to bring in up to 6 litres of wine, beer or spirits; 20 packs of cigarettes, or 25 cigars, or 200 g of tobacco and medicines for personal use. Goods imported into Mexico with a value of more than US$1000 (with the exception of computer equipment, where the limit is US$4000) have to be handled by an officially appointed agent. If you are carrying more than US$10,000 in cash you should declare it. There is no penalty but registration is required. Full details and latest updates are available at www.aduanas.sat.gob.mx.

Dress

Casual clothing is adequate for most occasions although men may need a jacket and tie in some restaurants. Dress conservatively in indigenous communities and small churches. Topless bathing is generally unacceptable.

Electricity

127 volts/60 Hz, US-style 2-pin plug.

Embassies and consulates

For details of Mexican embassies in the rest of the world, go to www.sre.gob.mx.
Australia, 14 Perth Av, Yarralumia, 2600 ACT, Canberra, T6273-3963, www.mexico.org.au.
Belize, 3 North Ring Rd, Belmopan, T822-0406.
Canada, 45 O'Connor St, Suite 1000, Ottawa, Ont, K1P 1A4, T613-233-8988, www.sre.gob.mx/canada.
Denmark, Bredgade 65, 1st floor 1260, Copenhagen, T3961-0500, www.sre.gob.mx/dinamarca.
France, 9 rue de Longchamp, 75116 Paris, T5370-2770, www.sre.gob.mx/francia.

Germany, Klingelhöferstrasse 3, 10785 Berlin, T30-269-3230, www.sre.gob.mx/alemania.
Holland, Nassauplein 28, 2585 EC, The Hague, T360-2900, www.embamex-nl.com.
Israel, 25 Hamared St, Trade Tower 5th floor, Tel Aviv 68125, T516-3938, www.sre.gob.mx/israel.
New Zealand, 185-187 Featherston St, level 2 (AMP Chambers), Wellington, T472-5555, www.sre.gob.mx/nuevazelandia.
Switzerland, Welpoststrasse 20, 5th floor, CH-3015, Berne, T357-4747, www.sre.gob.mx/suiza.
UK, 16 St George St, London, W1S 1FD, T020-7499-8586, www.sre.gob.mx/reinounido.
USA, 1911 Pennsylvania Av, NW, 20006 Washington DC, T202-728-1600, www.sre.gob.mx/eua.

Health

Social security hospitals are restricted to members, but will take visitors in emergencies; they are more up to date than the *Centros de Salud* and *Hospitales Civiles* found in most town centres, which are very cheap and open to everyone. A consultation in a private doctor's surgery may cost US$20-40.

Identification

ID is increasingly required when visiting offices or tourist sites within government buildings. It's handy to have some form of identification (*identificación* or *credencial*), a photocopied passport will usually do.

Internet

A list of useful websites is given on page 18. Every major town and these days most small villages now has at least one internet café, with more springing up daily. The better ones often cater for a wide range of internet services, including Skype. Prices vary from place to place but are normally around US$1.

Language

The official language of Mexico is Spanish. Outside of the main tourist centres, travelling without some knowledge of Spanish is a major hindrance. Adding to the challenges of communication, there are also numerous Mayan languages spoken in southern Mexico.

Media

The influential daily newspapers are: *Excelsior, Novedades, El Día, Uno Más Uno, El Universal, El Heraldo, La Jornada* (www.jornada.unam.mx, more to the left, with *Tiempo Libre*, listing cultural activities in Mexico City), *La Prensa* (a popular tabloid, with the largest circulation) and *El Nacional* (mouthpiece of the government). There are influential weekly magazines *Proceso, Siempre, Epoca* and *Quehacer Político*. The political satirical weekly is *Los Agachados. The Miami Herald* is stocked by most news-stands.

Money → *US$1=11.89 pesos (Aug 2011).*
The monetary unit is the Mexican peso, represented by '$' – the dollar sign – providing great potential for confusion, especially in popular tourist places where prices are higher and often quoted in US dollars (US$).

Exchange

US dollars cash can be easily changed at banks in all cities and towns and less economically at *casas de cambio*. Try to carry a mixture of large and small denominations; it can be hard to change notes of US$20 or higher in small villages. While it is possible to change the euro, sterling and other currencies, not all banks or *casas de cambio* will take them.

Traveller's cheques (TCs) from any well-known bank can be cashed in most towns if drawn in US dollars; TCs from other currencies are harder to cash. If you are stuck, branches of HSBC have been known to change other currencies. *Casas de cambio* are generally quicker than banks for

exchange transactions and stay open later; fees are not charged but their rates may not be as good. You may be asked to show some ID. Amex and Visa US dollar TCs are the easiest to change.

Transfer

If you need to make a transfer ask your bank if they can transfer direct to a Mexican bank without using an intermediary, which usually results in greater delays. Beware of short-changing at all times. **Western Union**, www.westernunion.com, have outlets throughout Mexico but the service is more expensive than a traditional bank wire.

Credit cards

ATMs are now found even in small towns, allowing you to travel without carrying large amounts of cash or TCs. **MasterCard**, **Visa** and **American Express** are widely accepted in Mexico either when paying for goods, withdrawing cash from ATMs (*cajero automático*) or obtaining cash over the counter from banks. There is often a 6% tax on the use of credit cards. For lost or stolen cards call: **MasterCard** T001-800-307-7309; **Visa** T001-800-847-2911.

Cost of living and travelling

Couples and groups will make good savings. A basic room is likely to set you back about US$15 on average, with occasionally cheaper prices available. Comfortable rooms start at around US$20. Meals start from US$8 a day for those on tight budgets and activities cost US$20 per day and upwards. Travel is expensive compared to the rest of Central America and you should definitely calculate costs into your budget (see Getting around, page 9). An impoverished couple might just survive on US$15 per person per day, but US$25 is a more realistic. Prices are considerably higher in resorts – seek out those places preferred by the locals.

Student cards

Although an international student (**ISIC**) card offers student discounts, only national Mexican student cards permit free entry to museums, archaeological sites, etc.

Opening hours

Banks Mon-Fri 0900-1330 (some stay open later), Sat 0900-1230.
Businesses 0900/1000-1300/1400, then 1400/1500-1900 or later. Business hours vary considerably according to the climate and local custom.

Photography

There is a charge of US$3-5 for the use of video cameras at historical sites. For professional camera equipment, including a tripod, the fee is much higher. Never take photos of indigenous people without prior permission.

Post

International service has improved and bright red mailboxes, found in many parts of the city, are reliable for letters. Poste Restante (*lista de correos* in Mexico) functions quite reliably, but you may have to ask under each of your names; mail is sent back after 10 days.

Safety

Mexico is generally a safe country to visit, although the usual precautions over personal safety should be taken. Cars are a prime target for theft; never leave possessions visible inside the car and park in hotel car parks after dark. Avoid travelling at night; if at all possible make journeys in daylight. Avoid lonely beaches, especially if you are a single woman. Other than the tourist police who are helpful, speak some English and who you'll only come across in more touristy areas, it is best to avoid the police if at all possible; they are rarely helpful and tend to make complicated situations even worse. Speaking Spanish is a great asset for avoiding rip-offs targeting gringos, especially short changing and overcharging (both rife).

Telephone → *Country code T+52.*

IDD T00; operator T020; international operator T090; directory enquiries T040. Most destinations have a 7-digit number and 3-digit regional code (Mexico City is an exception). The format of a number, depending on the type of call, should be as follows: **local** 7- or 8-digit phone number; **regional** long-distance access code (01) + regional code (2- or 3-digit code) + 7- or 8-digit number; **international** international direct-dialling code + country code + regional code + 7- or 8-digit number. Most public phones take phone cards only (**Ladatel**) costing 30 or 50 pesos from shops and news kiosks everywhere. Reverse-charge (collect) calls can be made from any blue public phone; say you want to *llamar por cobrar*. Pre-paid phone cards are expensive for international calls. Of other pre-paid cards, the best value are **Ekofon**, www.ekofon.com.

Time

Southern Mexico is in Central Standard Time (CST), 6 hrs behind GMT. Daylight Saving Time runs from the first Sun in Apr to the last Sun in Oct (when it is 5 hrs behind GMT).

Tipping

Normally 10-15%; the equivalent of US$0.25 per bag for porters, the equivalent of US$0.20 for bell boys, and nothing for a taxi driver unless some kind of exceptional service.

Tourist information

Tourist offices are listed throughout the text. In Europe, information is available in several different languages by calling T00-800-1111-2266. In North America call T1-800-446-3942.

Useful websites

Mexico's web presence is phenomenal, some of the reliable, informative and useful websites that have been round for a while include:

www.mexconnect.com General information.
www.mexperience.com Well-constructed site updated daily, with current affairs, feature articles and advice on travel in Mexico. Look out for the forum where comments from fellow travellers are exchanged.
www.sectur.gob.mx Tourism Secretariat's site, with less glossy links but equally comprehensive information.
www.visitmexico.com Mexico Tourist Board site, a comprehensive multilingual site with information on the entire country.

Visas and immigration

Virtually all international travellers require a passport to enter Mexico. Upon entry you will be issued a Mexican Tourist Card (FM-T), valid for up to 180 days. This must surrendered when leaving the country. If your stamp bears less than 180 days, you can extend it up to the limit at any **National Institute of Migration** office; you can find details at www.inm.gob.mx. To renew a tourist card by leaving the country, you must stay outside Mexico for at least 72 hrs. Take TCs or a credit card as proof of finance. At the border crossings with Belize and Guatemala, you may be refused entry into Mexico if you have less than US$200 (or US$350 for each month of intended stay, up to a maximum of 180 days). Likewise, if you are carrying more than US$10,000 in cash or TCs, you must declare it.

If a person **under 18** is travelling alone or with one parent, both parents' consent is required, certified by a notary or authorized by a consulate. A divorced parent must be able to show custody of a child. (These requirements are not always checked by immigration authorities and do not apply to all nationalities). Further details are available from any Mexican consulate (see page 15).

Weights and measures

The metric system is used.

Contents

Footprint features

At a glance

⊖ **Getting around** Buses between cities and minibus shuttles for shorter distances.

⟳ **Time required** 2-3 weeks to take in all the highlights.

☁ **Weather** Wet season runs May-Oct; dry season Nov-Apr. Temperatures generally mid-20°Cs.

✖ **When not to go** Resorts are packed in the summer.

Yucatán Peninsula

State of Campeche

Take time out to explore the State of Campeche. Colonial architecture is plentiful, there are several fortified convents and Campeche city itself was fortified to protect its citizens from pirate attacks. There are many archaeological sites, most demonstrating influences of Chenes-style architecture. Relax at the resorts of Sihoplaya and Seybaplaya while watching pelicans dive and iguanas scurry. You can try the beaches at Ciudad del Carmen, eat delicious red snapper and buy a cheap, but sturdy, Panama hat. The exhibits at several museums reflect the seafaring nature of the area and the pre-Conquest civilization that occupied these lands. The official government website is at www.campeche.gob.mx.

The word 'cocktail' is said to have originated in Campeche, where 17th-century English pirates enjoyed drinks adorned with palm fronds resembling cocks' tails.

Tabasco to Campeche → *For listings, see pages 29-33.*

There are two routes to Campeche from the neighbouring state of Tabasco: the inland Highway 186, via Escárcega, with two toll bridges (cost US$5), and the slightly longer coastal route through Ciudad del Carmen, Highway 180; both converge at Champotón, 66 km south of Campeche. Highway 186 passes Villahermosa's modern international airport and runs fast and smooth in a sweeping curve 115 km east to the Palenque turn-off at Playas del Catazajá; beyond, off the highway, is **Emiliano Zapata** (fiesta 26 October), a busy cattle centre, with a Pemex station.

Francisco Escárcega → *Phone code: 982.*

Escárcega is a major hub for travellers on their way south to the states of Tabasco and Chiapas, north to Mérida in the state of Yucatán, east to Maya sites in Campeche and Quintana Roo states, and further east to the city of Chetumal. The town itself is not particularly enticing, set on a busy highway with a dusty wild west atmosphere. If stuck here overnight, there are a couple of hotels, a bank and several cheap restaurants.

Coast road to Campeche → *For listings, see pages 29-33.*

Although Highway 180 via Ciudad del Carmen is narrow, crumbling into the sea in places and usually ignored by tourists intent on visiting Palenque, this journey is beautiful and more interesting than the fast toll road inland to Campeche. The road threads its way from Villahermosa 78 km north through marshland and rich cacao, banana and coconut plantations, passing turnings to tiny coastal villages with palm-lined but otherwise mediocre beaches. It finally leads to the river port of **Frontera**, where Graham Greene began the research journey in 1938 that led to the publication of *The Lawless Roads* and later to *The Power and the Glory*. The **Feria Guadalupana** is held from 3-13 December, with an agricultural show, bullfights, *charreadas* and regional dances.

The road touches the coast at the Tabasco/Campeche state border. It then runs east beside a series of lakes (superb birdwatching) to the fishing village of **Zacatal** (93 km), at the entrance to the **Laguna de Términos** (named for the first Spanish expedition, which thought it had reached the end of the 'island' of Yucatán). Just before Zacatal is the lighthouse of **Xicalango**, an important pre-Columbian trading centre. Cortés landed near here in 1519 on his way to Veracruz and was given 20 female slaves, including 'La Malinche', the indigenous princess baptized as Doña Marina who, as the Spaniards' interpreter, played an important role in the Conquest. A bridge crosses the lake's mouth to Ciudad del Carmen.

Ciudad del Carmen → *Phone code: 938.*
This is the hot, bursting-at-the-seams principal oil port of the region. The site was established in 1588 by a pirate named McGregor as a lair from which to raid Spanish shipping; it was infamous until the pirates were wiped out by Alfonso Felipe de Andrade in 1717, who named the town after its patroness, the Virgen del Carmen.

Most streets in the centre are numbered; even numbers generally run west-east, and odd south-north. Calle 20 is the seafront *malecón* and the road to the airport and university is Calle 31. There's a **tourist office** ① *at the main plaza, near the seafront Malecón, 0800-1500.*

The attractive, cream-coloured **cathedral** (Parroquia de la Virgen del Carmen), begun 1856, is notable for its stained glass. **La Iglesia de Jesús** (1820) opposite Parque Juárez is surrounded by elegant older houses. Nearby is the Barrio del Guanal, the oldest residential quarter, with the church of the **Virgen de la Asunción** (1815) and houses with spacious balconies and tiles brought from Marseilles.

There are several good beaches with restaurants and watersports, the most scenic being Playa Caracol (southeast of the centre) and Playa Norte, which has extensive white sand and safe bathing. Fishing excursions can be arranged through the **Club de Pesca** ① *Nelo Manjárrez, T938-382 0073, at Calle 40 and Calle 61.* Coastal lagoons are rich in tarpon (*sábalo*) and bonefish. The town's patroness is honoured with a cheerful fiesta each year between 15 and 30 June.

Maya sites in south Campeche → *For listings, see pages 29-33.*

Calakmul
① *Daily 0800-1700, US$3.70, cars US$4, entrance to biosphere reserve US$4.*
Three hundred kilometres southeast from Campeche town, and a further 60 km off the main Escárcega–Chetumal road, the ruins of Calakmul are only accessible by car. The site has been the subject of much attention in recent years, due to the previously concealed scale of the place. It is now believed to be one of the largest archaeological sites in Mesoamerica, and certainly the biggest of all the Maya cities, with somewhere in the region of 10,000 buildings in total, many of them as yet unexplored. There is evidence that Calakmul was begun in 300 BC, and continually added to until AD 800. At the centre of the site is the Gran Plaza, overlooked by a pyramid whose base covers 2 ha of ground.

One of the buildings grouped around the **Gran Plaza** is believed, due to its curious shape and location, to have been designed for astronomical observation. The **Gran Acrópolis**, the largest of all the structures, is divided into two sections: **Plaza Norte**, with the ball court, was used for ceremonies; **Plaza Sur** was used for public activities. The scale of the site is vast, and many of the buildings are still under excavation, which means that information on Calakmul's history is continually being updated. To reach Calakmul, take Route 186 until Km 95, then turn off at Conhuás, where a paved road leads to the site, 60 km.

Xpujil → *Phone code: 983.*
① *Tue-Sun 0800-1700, US$3.40, US$3 to use a camcorder.*
The name means a type of plant similar to a cattail. The architectural style is known as Río Bec, characterized by heavy masonry towers simulating pyramids and temples, usually found rising in pairs at the ends of elongated buildings. The main building at Xpujil features an unusual set of three towers, with rounded corners and steps that are so steep they are unscalable, suggesting they may have been purely decorative. The façade features the open jaws of an enormous reptile in profile on either side of the main entrance, possibly representing Itzamná, the Maya god of creation. Xpujil's main period of activity was AD 500-750; it began to go into decline around 1100. Major excavation on the third structure was done as recently as 1993, and there are still many unexcavated buildings dotted about the site. It can be very peaceful and quiet in the early mornings, compared with the throng of tourist activity at the more accessible sites such as Chichén Itzá and Uxmal. To get there, see Transport, page 32.

The tiny village of Xpujil, on the Chetumal–Escárcega highway, is conveniently located for the three sets of ruins in this area, Xpujil, Becán and Chicanná. There are two hotels and a couple of shops. Guided tours to the more remote sites, such as Calakmul and Río Bec, can be organized through either of the two hotels, costing about US$20-30 per person for the whole day.

Becán → *Phone code: 996.*
① *Daily 0800-1700, US$3.70.*
Seven kilometres west of Xpujil, Becán is another important site in the Río Bec style. Its most outstanding feature is a moat, now dry, which surrounds the entire city and is believed to be one of the oldest defence systems in Mesoamerica. Seven entrance gates cross the moat to the city. The large variety of buildings on the site are a strange combination of decorative towers and fake temples, as well as structures used as shrines and palaces. The twin towers, typical of the Río Bec style, feature on the main structure, set on a pyramid-shaped base supporting a cluster of buildings that seem to have been used for many different functions.

Chicanná → *Phone code: 981.*
① *Daily 0800-1700. US$3.40.*
Located 12 km from Xpujil, Chicanná was named upon its discovery in 1966 in reference to Structure II: *chi* (mouth), *can* (serpent) and *ná* (house), 'House of the Serpent's Mouth'. Due to its dimensions and location, Chicanná is considered to have been a small residential centre for the rulers of the ancient regional capital of Becán. It was occupied during the late pre-Classic period (300 BC-AD 250); the final stages of activity at the site

have been dated to the post-Classic era (AD 1100). Typical of the Río Bec style are numerous representations of the Maya god Itzamná, or Earth Mother. One of the temples has a dramatic entrance in the shape of a monster's mouth, with fangs jutting out over the lintel and more fangs lining the access stairway. A taxi will take you from Xpujil bus stop to Becán and Chicanná for US$10, including waiting time.

Hormiguero
① *Daily 0800-1700, US$2.50.*
Twenty kilometres southwest of Xpujil, Hormiguero is the site of one of the most important buildings in the Río Bec region, whose elaborate carvings on the façade show a fine example of the serpent's-mouth entrance, with huge fangs and a gigantic eye.

Río Bec
Río Bec is south off the main highway, some 10 km further along the road to Chetumal. Although the site gave its name to the architectural style seen in this area, there are better examples of it at the ruins listed above. Río Bec is a cluster of several smaller sites, all of which are very difficult to reach without a guide.

Champotón
Back near the west coast of Campeche state, Route 261 runs 86 km due north from Escárcega through dense forest to the Gulf of Mexico, where it joins the coastal route at Champotón, a relaxed but run-down fishing and shrimping port spread along the banks of Río Champotón. In pre-Hispanic times it was an important trading link between Guatemala and Central Mexico; Toltec and Maya mingled here, followed by the Spaniards; in fact blood was shed here when Francisco Hernández de Córboba was fatally wounded in a skirmish with the inhabitants in 1517. The remnants of a 1719 fort built as a defence against the pirates who frequently raided this coast can be seen the south side of town. The Feast of the Immaculate Conception (8 December) is celebrated with a joyous festival lasting several days.

Sihoplaya and Seybaplaya → *Phone code: 982.*
Continuing north, Highways 180 and 261 are combined for 17 km until the latter darts off east on its way to Edzná and Hopelchen (bypassing Campeche, should this be desired). A 66-km toll *autopista*, paralleling Highway 180, just inland from the southern outskirts of Champotón to Campeche, is much quicker than the old highway. Champotón and Seybaplaya are bypassed. But from the old Highway 180, narrow and slow with speed bumps, you can reach the resort of **Sihoplaya** (regular buses from Campeche US$1). A short distance further north is the larger resort of **Seybaplaya**. This is an attractive place where fishermen mend nets and pelicans dry their wings along the beach. On the highway is the open-air **Restaurant Veracruz**, serving delicious red snapper (fresh fish at the seafront public market is also good value), but in general there is little to explore. Only the **Balneario Payucán** at the north end of the bay makes a special trip worthwhile; this is probably the closest decent beach to Campeche (33 km), although a little isolated, as the water and sand get filthier as one nears the state capital. Nevertheless, there is still much reef life to enjoy.

Campeche → *For listings, see pages 29-33. Phone code: 981.*

Campeche's charm is neatly hidden behind traffic-blocked streets, but once inside the city walls it reveals itself as a good place to break your journey out to the Yucatán. At the end of the 20th century, the town of Campeche was declared a World Heritage Site by UNESCO. The clean streets of brightly painted houses give the town a relaxed Caribbean feel. The Malecón is a beautiful promenade where people stroll, cycle, walk and relax in the evening in the light of the setting sun.

Ins and outs

Like many Yucatán towns, Campeche's streets in the Old Town are numbered rather than named. Even numbers run north/south beginning at Calle 8 (no one knows why) near the Malecón, east to Calle 18 inside the walls; odd numbers run east (inland) from Calle 51 in the north to Calle 65 in the south. Most of the points of interest are within this compact area. A full circuit of the walls is a long walk; buses marked 'Circuito Baluartes' provide a regular service around the perimeter.

The **state tourist office** ① *T981-811 9229, www.campechetravel.com, daily 0800-2100*, is on the Malecón in front of the Palacio de Gobierno (walk down Calle 61 towards the sea). There is another smaller **tourist office** ① *on the northeastern corner of the zócalo, next to the cathedral, daily 0900-2100*. For a good orientation take the Centro Histórico tour, a regular **tourist tram** ① *daily on the hour from 0900-1200 and 1700-2000, 45 mins, US$7.50, English and Spanish spoken*, running from the main plaza.

Background

Highway 180 enters the city as the Avenida Resurgimiento, passing either side of the huge **Monumento al Resurgimiento**, a stone torso holding aloft the Torch of Democracy. Originally the trading village of Ah Kim Pech, it was here that the Spaniards, under Francisco Hernández de Córdoba, first disembarked on Mexican soil (22 March 1517) to replenish their water supply. For fear of being attacked by the native population, they quickly left, only to be attacked later by the locals further south in Champotón, where they were forced to land by appalling weather conditions at sea. It was not until 1540 that Francisco de Montejo managed to conquer Ah Kim Pech, founding the city of Campeche on 4 October 1541, after failed attempts in 1527 and again in 1537. The export of local dyewoods, *chicle*, timber and other valuable cargoes soon attracted the attention of most of the famous buccaneers, who constantly raided the port from their bases on Isla del Carmen, then known as the Isla de Tris. Combining their fleets for one momentous swoop, they fell upon Campeche on 9 February 1663, wiped out the city and slaughtered its inhabitants. Five years later the Crown began fortifying the site, the first Spanish colonial settlement to be completely walled. Formidable bulwarks, 3 m thick and 'a ship's height', and eight bastions (*baluartes*) were built in the next 36 years. All these fortifications soon put a stop to pirate attacks and Campeche prospered as one of only two Mexican ports (the other was Veracruz) to have had the privilege of conducting international trade. After Mexican Independence from Spain, the city declined into an obscure fishing and logging town. Only with the arrival of a road from the 'mainland' in the 1950s and the oil boom of the 1970s has Campeche begun to see visitors in any numbers, attracted by its historical monuments and relaxed atmosphere (*campechano* has come to mean an easy-going, pleasant person).

Sights

Of the original walls, seven of the *baluartes* and an ancient fort (now rather dwarfed by two big white hotels on the seafront) remain. Some house museums (see below).

The heart of the city is the zócalo, where the austere Franciscan **cathedral** (1540-1705) has an elaborately carved façade; inside is the Santo Entierro (Holy Burial), a sculpture of Christ on a mahogany sarcophagus with a silver trim. There is plenty of shade under the trees in the zócalo, and a small pagoda with a snack bar.

Right in front of the zócalo is the **Baluarte de Nuestra Señora de la Soledad**, the central bulwark of the city walls, from where you can do a walking tour of the **Circuito Baluartes**, the remains of the city walls. Heading east, you will come to the **Puerta del Mar**, formerly the entrance for those permitted to enter the city from the sea, which used to come up to this point. Next along the *Circuito* is a pair of modern buildings, the **Palacio**

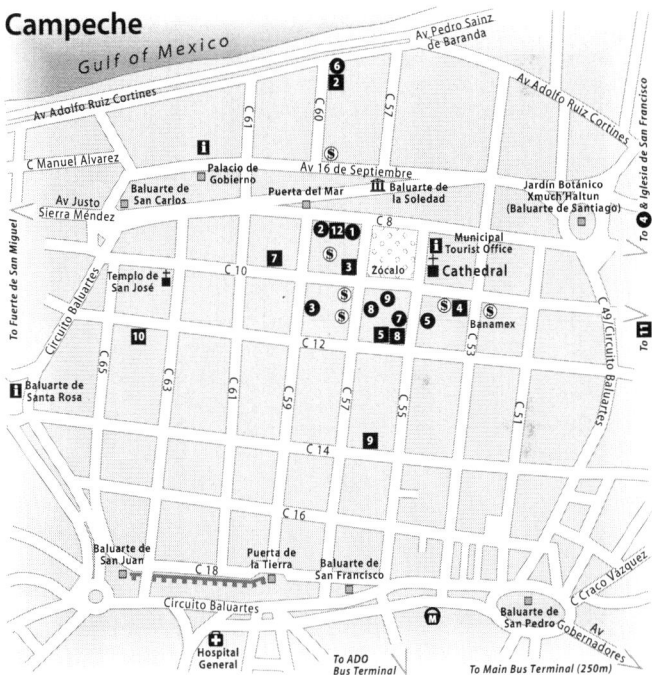

Campeche

100 metres
100 yards

Sleeping	La Posada del Angel 4	Iguana Azul 5
América 7	Monkey Hostal Campeche 3	Lafitte's 6
Colonial 9	Reforma 12	La Parroquia 7
Best Western Hotel	Regis 5	La Pigua 4
del Mar 2		Tulum 3
Francis Drake 10	Eating	Turix Café 8
Hostal San Carlos 11	Campeche 1	Marganzo 2
La Parroquia 8	Casa Vieja Los Arcos 9	

de Gobierno and the **Congreso.** The latter looks like a flying saucer, and makes for a bizarre sight when viewed with the 17th-century **Baluarte de San Carlos** in the background. Baluarte de San Carlos now houses a museum. Heading west on the continuation of the *Circuito*, you will come to **Templo de San José**, on Calle 10, an impressive baroque church with a beautifully tiled façade. It has been de-consecrated, and is now an educational centre. Back on to the *Circuito*, you will next reach the **Baluarte de Santa Rosa**, now the home of the tourist information office. Next is **Baluarte de San Juan**, from which a large chunk of the old city wall still extends, protecting you from the noisy traffic on the busy road beyond it. The wall connects with **Puerta de la Tierra** ① *Tue, Fri and Sat 2000 (for information, contact the tourist office)*, where a *Luz y Sonido* (Light and Sound) show takes place, US$4. The continuation of the *Circuito* will take you past the **Baluarte de San Francisco**, and then past the market, just outside the line of the city walls. **Baluarte de San Pedro** flanks the northeast corner of the city centre, and now houses a museum. The *circuito* runs down to the northwest tip of the old city, where the **Baluarte de Santiago** houses the Botanical Gardens.

Further from the city walls is the **Batería de San Luis**, 4 km south from the centre along the coast road. This was once a lookout post to catch pirates as they approached the city from a distance. The **Fuerte de San Miguel**, 600 m inland, is now a museum. A 20-minute walk along Avenida Miguel Alemán from Baluarte de Santiago is the **San Francisco** church, 16th century with wooden altars painted in vermilion and white. Nearby are the **Portales de San Francisco**, a beautifully restored old entrance to the city, with several good restaurants in its shadow.

The **Museo de la Escultura Maya** ① *Baluarte de Nuestra Señora de la Soledad, Tue-Sun, 0800-1930, US$2.50*, has three well-laid-out rooms of Maya stelae and sculpture. **Jardín Botánico Xmuch'Haltun** ① *Baluarte de Santiago, Tue-Sun 0900-1600*, is a small, but perfectly formed collection of tropical plants and flowers in a peaceful setting. The **Fuerte de San Miguel** ① *Tue-Sun 0900-1930, US$2.50*, on the Malecón 4 km southwest, is the most atmospheric of the forts (complete with drawbridge and a moat said to have once contained either crocodiles or skin-burning lime, take your pick!); it houses the **Museo Arqueológico**, with a well-documented display of pre-Columbian exhibits including jade masks and black funeral pottery from Calakmul and recent finds from Jaina.

Around Campeche

Lerma is virtually a small industrial suburb of Campeche, with large shipyards and fish-processing plants; the afternoon return of the shrimping fleet is a colourful sight. The **Fiesta de Polk Kekén** is held on 6 January, with traditional dances. The nearest decent beaches are at Seybaplaya (see page 23), 20 km south of Campeche. There, the beaches are clean and deserted; take your own food and drink as there are no facilities. Crowded, rickety buses marked 'Lerma' or 'Playa Bonita' run from Campeche, US$1, 8 km.

Maya sites east of Campeche → *For listings, see pages 29-33.*

A number of city remains (mostly in the Chenes architectural style) are scattered throughout the rainforest and scrub to the east of Campeche; little excavation work has been done and most receive few visitors. Getting to them by the occasional bus service is possible in many cases, but return trips can be tricky. The alternatives are one of the tours run by some luxury hotels and travel agencies in Campeche (see Tour operators, page 31) or renting a vehicle (preferably with high clearance) in Campeche or Mérida. Whichever way you travel, you are strongly advised to carry plenty of drinking water.

Edzná

ⓘ *Tue-Sun 0800-1700, US$3; local guides available.*

The closest site to the state capital is Edzná ('House of Grimaces'), reached by the highway east to Cayal, then a right turn onto Highway 261, a distance of 61 km. A paved shortcut southeast through China and Poxyaxum (good road) cuts off 11 km; follow Avenida Nacozari out along the railway track. Gracefully situated in a lovely, tranquil valley with thick vegetation on either side, Edzná was a huge ceremonial centre, occupied from about 600 BC to AD 200, built in the simple Chenes style mixed with Puuc, Classic and other influences. The centrepiece is the magnificent, 30-m-tall, 60-sq-m **Temple of the Five Storeys**, a stepped pyramid with four levels of living quarters for the priests and a shrine and altar at the top; 65 steep steps lead up from the Central Plaza. Opposite is the **Paal U'na**, Temple of the Moon. Excavations are being carried out on the scores of lesser temples by Guatemalan refugees under the direction of Mexican archaeologists, but most of Edzná's original sprawl remains hidden away under thick vegetation. Imagination is still needed to picture the network of irrigation canals and holding basins built by the Maya along the valley below sea level. Some of the stelae remain in position (two large stone faces with grotesquely squinting eyes are covered by a thatched shelter); others can be seen in various Campeche museums. There is also a good example of a *sacbé* (sacred road). There is a small *comedor* at the entrance. Edzná is well worth a visit especially in July, when a Maya ceremony to honour Chac is held, to encourage or to celebrate the arrival of the rains (exact date varies). To get there see Transport, page 32 .

Hochob

ⓘ *Daily 0800-1700, US$2.70.*

Of the more remote and less-visited sites beyond Edzná, Hochob and Dzibilnocac are the best choices for the non-specialist. Hochob is reached by turning right at Hopelchén on Highway 261, 85 km east of Campeche. This quiet town has an impressive fortified 16th-century church but only one hotel. From here a narrow paved road leads 41 km south to the village of **Dzibalchén**. Don Willem Chan will guide tourists to Hochob (he also rents bikes for US$3.50 per day), helpful, speaks English. Directions can be obtained from the church here (run by Americans); you need to travel 18 km southwest on a good dirt road (no public transport, hopeless quagmire in the rainy season) to the village of Chenko, where locals will show the way (4 km through the jungle). Bear left when the road forks; it ends at a small *palapa* and, from here, the ruins are 1 km uphill with a magnificent view over the surrounding forest. Hochob once covered a large area but, as at Edzná, only the hilltop ceremonial centre (the usual Plaza surrounded by elaborately decorated temple buildings) has been properly excavated; although many of these are mounds of rubble, the site is perfect for contemplating deserted, yet accessible Maya ruins in solitude and silence. The one-room temple to the right (north) of the plaza is the most famous structure: deep-relief patterns of stylized snakes moulded in stucco across its façade were designed to resemble a mask of the ferocious rain god Chac. A door serves as the mouth. A fine reconstruction of the building is on display at the Museo de

Antropología in Mexico City. Early morning second-class buses serve Dzibalchén, but, returning to Campeche later in the day is often a matter of luck.

Dzibilnocac
ⓘ *Daily 0800-1700, free.*

Twenty kilometres northeast of Dzibalchén at Iturbide, this site is one of the largest in Chenes territory. Only three temples have been excavated here (many pyramidal mounds in the forest and roadside *milpas*); the first two are in a bad state of preservation, but the third is worth the visit: a unique narrow edifice with rounded corners and remains of a stucco façade, primitive reliefs and another grim mask of Chac on the top level. Much of the stonework from the extensive site is used by local farmers for huts and fences. A bus leaves Campeche at 0800, three hours, return 1245, 1345 and 1600, US$3.35. If driving your own vehicle, well-marked 'km' signs parallel the rocky road to Iturbide (no accommodation); bear right around the tiny zócalo and its attendant yellow church and continue (better to walk in the wet season) for 50 m, where the right branch of a fork leads to the ruins. Other sites in the region require 4WD transport and appeal mostly to archaeologists.

Becal
Becal is the centre for weaving Panama hats, here called *jipis* (pronounced 'hippies') and ubiquitous throughout the Yucatán. Many of the town's families have workshops in cool, moist backyard underground caves, which are necessary for keeping moist and pliable the shredded leaves of the *jipijapa* palm from which the hats are made. Most vendors give the visitor a tour of their workshop, but are quite zealous in their sales pitches. Prices are better for *jipis* and other locally woven items (cigarette cases, shoes, belts, etc) in the **Centro Artesanal, Artesanías de Becaleña** ⓘ *Calle 30 No 210*, than in the shops near the plaza, where the hat is honoured by a hefty sculpture of three concrete *sombreros*! More celebrations take place on 20 May during the **Feria del Jipi**.

State of Campeche listings

For Sleeping and Eating price codes and other relevant information, see pages 12-13.

● Sleeping

Francisco Escárcega *p20*
\$\$ Escárcega, Justo Sierra 86, T982-824 0187, around the corner from the bus terminal (turn left twice). Clean, bath, parking, hot water, good restaurant, small garden.
\$\$ María Isabel, Justo Sierra 127, T982-824 0045. A/c, restaurant, comfortable, back rooms noisy from highway.
\$\$ Motel Akim Pech, T982-824 0240, on Villahermosa highway. A/c or fans and bath, reasonable rooms, restaurant in motel, another across the street, and a Pemex station opposite.

Coast road to Campeche *p20*
\$\$ San Agustín, Pino Suárez, Frontera, T913-332 0037. Very basic, fan, no mosquito net.
\$ Chichén Itzá, Aldama 671, Frontera, T913-332 0097. Not very clean, fan, shower, hot water.

Ciudad del Carmen *p21*
Hotel accommodation is generally poor value and can be difficult to come by Mon-Thu; book in advance and arrive early. You'll find a handful of 'economical' hotels opposite the ADO bus station.
\$\$\$ EuroHotel, Calle 22 No 208, T938-382 3044, reganem@prodigy.net.mx. Large and modern, 2 restaurants, pool, a/c, disco, built to accommodate the flow of Pemex traffic.
\$\$ Lino's, Calle 31 No 132, T938-382 0788 A/c, pool, restaurant, also has 10 RV spaces with electricity hook-ups.
\$ Zacarías, Calle 24 No 58B, T938-382 3506. Modern, some cheaper rooms with fans, brighter a/c rooms are better value. Recommended.

Campeche *p24, map p25*
In general, prices are high. Beware of over-charging and, if driving, find a secure car park.
\$\$\$ Best Western Hotel Del Mar, Av Ruiz Cortines 51, T981-811 9191, www.delmar hotel.com.mx. 5-star hotel on the waterfront, has pleasant rooms with seaview and balconies, all mod cons and free Wi-Fi in the rooms. Pool, gym, good bar and restaurant.
\$\$\$ Hotel Francis Drake, Calle 12 No 207, between Calle 63 and Calle 65, T981-811 5626, www.hotelfrancisdrake.com. Classy colonial hotel with well-equipped rooms, restaurant, bar and a good business centre.
\$\$ América, Calle 10 252, T981-816 4588, www.hotelamericacampeche.com. This centrally located hotel is clean, tidy and well staffed. The rooms here have Wi-Fi and breakfast is included in the price. An attractive mid-range option.
\$\$ El Regis, Calle 12 No 148, between 55 and 57, T981-816 3175. Housed in a lovely old colonial building, the reception is a bit dark and dingy, but the hotel sports clean, spacious rooms and a stylish chequered floor.
\$\$ La Posada Del Angel, Calle 10 No 307, T981-816 7718 (on the side entrance of the cathedral). Clean, carpeted, comfortable rooms, some without windows, some with a/c. Friendly and recommended.
\$ Hostal San Carlos, Calle 10, No 255, Barrio de Guadalupe, a few blocks out of town, T981-816 5158, info@hostelcampeche. com.mx. Private rooms and dorms, continental breakfast included. Well-kept hostel with hot water, internet, currency exchange, laundry service and bike rental.
\$ Hotel Colonial, Calle 14 No 122, between Calle 55 and 57, T981-816 2630. Rooms have fans or a/c (more expensive) and hot water. A nice old colonial building, this quaint old hotel open since 1946, is living up to its name. Slightly scruffy, but very friendly.

$ Hotel Reforma, Calle 8 No 257, between Calle 57 and 59, T981-816 4464. Has a/c, hot water, TV and internet. A bit grotty, but right in the centre just a minute from the main plaza.

$ La Parroquia, Calle 55, between 10 y 12, T981-816 2530, www.hostalparroquia.com. 3 dorms and rooms in one of Campeche's historic buildings. Services include free breakfast, kitchen, internet, bike rental book exchange, TV room with DVDs, and a tranquil terrace complete with sun loungers.

$ Monkey Hostel Campeche, Calle 57 No 10, overlooking the zócalo, T981-811 6605, www.hostalcampeche.com. Dorms and private rooms. There are lockers, laundry, internet, bike hire, kitchen and book exchange. Price includes breakfast and can arrange local tours. Luggage storage US$2.

Camping

Club Náutica, 15 km south of town, on the highway out of Campeche, Km 180, T981-816 7545. Big campsite with good facilities. Good spot for a few days.

🍴 Eating

Francisco Escárcega *p20*

There are few places used to serving tourists, but there is a good and cheap *lonchería* opposite the bus terminal.

$$ Titanic, corner of the main highway and the road to the train station (1st turning on the right after turning right out of the bus terminal). For a more expensive meal with a/c.

Ciudad del Carmen *p21*

$$ El Kiosco Calle 33 s/n, between Calle 20 and 22, in **Hotel del Parque** with view of zócalo. Modest prices, eggs, chicken, seafood and Mexican dishes.

$$-$ El Pavo, tucked away down Calle 36A, in Col Guadalupe. This superb, family-run restaurant serves excellent seafood dishes at cheap prices. Very popular with the locals.

$$-$ La Fuente, Calle 20. 24-hr snack bar with view of the Laguna.

$ La Mesita, outdoor stand across from the old ferry landing. Well-prepared shrimp, seafood cocktails, extremely popular all day.

Cafés

There are several tiny cafés along the pedestrian walkway (Calle 33) near the zócalo.

Café Vadillo, Calle 33. The 'best coffee in town'.

Casa Blanca, Calle 20, between Calle 29 and 27. This popular and modern café-bar overlooks the seafront *malecón*. It serves filter coffee, cappuccinos and espressos.

Mercado Central, Calle 20 and 37, not far northwest of zócalo. Inexpensive snacks are available in the thriving market.

Campeche *p24, map p25*

Campeche is known for its seafood, especially *camarones* (large shrimps), *esmedregal* (black snapper) and *pan de cazón* (baby hammerhead shark sandwiched between corn tortillas with black beans). Food stands in the market serve *tortas*, tortillas, *panuchos* and *tamales* but hygiene standards vary widely; barbecued venison is also a marketplace speciality.

$$$-$$ Casa Vieja Los Arcos, Calle 10, No 319A, on the zócalo, T981-100 5522. Beautiful balcony dining on top of the portales overlooking the main plaza. Specializes in local dishes, including *camarones*. Romantic setting.

$$$-$$ Lafitte's Restaurant, inside **Hotel del Mar**. Pirate-themed restaurant with excellent Mexican dishes and good bar. There's a terrace overlooking the sea for outdoor dining. Recommended.

$$ La Pigua, Av Miguel Alemán 179A, www.lapigua.com.mx. A locally renowned, clean, modern restaurant that specializes in seafood. It's open for lunch and dinner, and there's a pleasant garden setting.

$$ RestauranteTulum, Calle 59 No 9, between Calle 10 and 12. This friendly, modern restaurant employs emerging talent from Campeche's gastronomic college. The menu is varied and international, offering white and red meats, baguettes, crêpes and salads. Open from lunchtime.

$$-$ Iguana Azul, Calle 55, between Calle 10 and Calle 12. Bar with live music and dancing, snacks and good selection of drinks.

$$-$ La Parroquia, Calle 55 No 8, part of the hotel with the same name. This busy locals' joint – staffed by smartly attired and friendly waiters – is open 24 hrs. It serves meat, fish and Mexican staples. Good breakfasts and a decent and economical *menú del día*. Free Wi-Fi. Recommended.

$$-$ Marganzo, Calle 8. An elegant and widely respected fine-dining establishment. It boasts a very interesting menu of seafood and *comida típica*, and regularly lays on music with a trio of musicians and regional dancing.

$$-$ Restaurant Campeche, right on the zócalo, opposite the cathedral, has an extensive menu, big portions and is very good value.

$ Turix, Calle 57 between Calle 10 and 12. Arts and crafts centre combined with gourmet. This little cute café and art space a short hop from the zócalo does a variety of salads, sandwiches and good desserts. Art and crafts for sale.

⊛ Festivals and events

Campeche *p24, map p25*
Feb/Mar Good **Carnival**.
7 Aug State holiday.
Sep Feria de San Román, 2nd fortnight.
4-13 Oct Fiesta de San Francisco.

Maya sites east of Campeche *p26*
13-17 Apr A traditional **Honey and Corn Festival** is held in Holpechén.
3 May Día de la Santa Cruz.

⊙ Shopping

Campeche *p24, map p25*
Excellent cheap Panama hats *(jipis)*, finely and tightly woven so that they retain their shape even when crushed into your luggage (within reason); cheaper at the source in Becal. Handicrafts are generally cheaper than in Mérida. There are souvenir shops along Calle 8, such as **Artesanía Típica Naval**, Calle 8 No 259, with exotic bottled fruit like *nance* and *marañón*. Many high-quality craft items are available from the **Exposición** in the Baluarte San Pedro, and **Casa de Artesanías Tukulná**, Calle 10 No 333, between C59 and C31, open daily 0900-2000.

The **market**, from which most local buses depart, is beside Alameda Park at the south end of Calle 57. Plenty of bargains here. Try the ice cream, although preferably from a shop rather than a barrow. **Super 10** supermarket behind the post office has an excellent cheap bakery inside.

▲ Activities and tours

Campeche *p24, map p25*
Tour operators
Intermar Campeche, Av 16 de Septiembre 128, T981-816 9006, www.travel2mexico. com. Tours, ground transport, flights and car rental.
Viajes Chicanná, Av Augustín Melgar, Centro Comercial Triángulo del Sol, Local 12, T981-811 3503. Flight bookings to Cuba, Miami and Central America.
Viajes del Golfo, Calle 10 No 250 D, T981-816 1745, viajesdelgolfo@hotmail.com. Domestic and international flights; tours to archaeological sites.
Viajes Xtampak Tours, Calle 57 No 14, T981-816 6473, www.xtampak.com. Daily transport to ruins including Edzná, Calakmul, Uxmal and Palenque – they'll collect you from your hotel with 24 hrs' notice. There's a discount for groups and guide services at an extra cost. Recommended.

Tabasco to Campeche *p20*
Bus Buses from Emiliano Zapata, all **ADO**. To **Tenosique**, almost hourly, 1½ hrs US$3. To **Villahermosa**, frequent services, 2½ hrs, US$7. To **Mérida**, 0900, 1120, 1500, 2215, 7 hrs, US$23.50. To **Escárcega**, 0900, 1500, 2 hrs, US$7.50. To **Chetumal**, 2100, 6 hrs, US$20.

Francisco Escárcega *p20*
Bus Most buses from Chetumal or Campeche drop you off at the 2nd-class terminal on the main highway. To buy tickets, you have to wait until the outgoing bus has arrived; sit near the ticket office and wait for them to call out your destination, then join the scrum at the ticket office. There is an **ADO** terminal west of the 2nd-class terminal, a 20-min walk. From there, 1st-class buses go to **Palenque**, 0410, 0630, 1250, 2335, 3 hrs, US$10. To **Chetumal**, frequent services, 4 hrs, US$13. To **Campeche**, frequent services, 2 hrs, US$7.50. From the 2nd-class terminal, there are buses to **Campeche**, 16 a day, 2½ hrs, US$5.60. To **Chetumal**, 3 a day, 4 hrs, US$11. To **Playas de Catazajá**, connecting with *colectivos* to **Palenque**, frequent, US$5. To **Villahermosa**, 12 a day, 4 hrs, US$12.50. *Colectivos* to **Palenque** leave from outside the 2nd-class terminal, US$5.50. From 1st class terminal to **Mérida**, frequent, 4½ hrs, US$16.50.

Ciudad del Carmen *p21*
Air
Carmen's airport (**CME**, 5 km east of the plaza) currently only has direct flights to **Mexico City**, from where there are connections to the rest of the country.

Bus
The **ADO** bus terminal is some distance from the centre. Take bus or *colectivo* marked 'Renovación' or 'ADO'; they leave from around the zócalo. There are frequent **ADO** and **ATS** services to **Campeche**, 2½-3 hrs, US$11. To **Mérida**, 6 hrs, US$21. To **Villahermosa** via the coast, 3 hrs, US$9, where connections can be made to **Palenque**. Buses also travel via **Escárcega**, where you can connect to **Chetumal** and **Belize**.

Car
Car hire **Budget**, Calle 31 No 117, T938-382 0908. **Auto-Rentas del Carmen**, Calle 33 No 121, T938-382 2376.

Xpujil *p22*
Bus 2nd-class buses from **Chetumal** and **Escárcega** stop on the highway in the centre of Xpujil, some 800 m east of the 2 hotels. There are 4 buses a day to **Escárcega**, between 1030 and 1500, 3 hrs, US$6. 8 buses a day to **Chetumal**, 2 hrs, US$5. Change at Escárcega for buses to **Palenque** or **Campeche**. 1st-class buses will not stop at Xpujil.

Campeche *p24, map p25*
Air
Modern, efficient airport (**CPE**) on Porfirio, 10 km northeast. **AeroMéxico** direct daily to **Mexico City**, T981-816 3109. If on a budget, walk 100 m down service road (Av Aviación) to Av Nacozari, turn right (west) and wait for 'China–Campeche' bus to zócalo.

Bus
The easiest way to reach **Edzna** is on a tourist minibus. They depart hourly and operators include **Xtampak**, Calle 57 No 14, between Calle 10 and 12, T981-812 8655, xtampac_7@ hotmail.com, US$21.50 (prices drop depending on number of passengers); and **Transportadora Turística Jade**, Av Díaz Ordaz No 67, T981-827 4885, Jade_tour@ hotmail.com, US$14. To get there on public transport, catch a morning bus to Pich and ask to be let out at Edzna – it's a 15-min walk from the highway. Ask the driver about return schedules, as services are quite infrequent and subject to change. There's no

accommodation at Edzná and hitchhiking isn't recommended. Buses to **Seybaplaya** leave from the tiny Cristo Rey terminal opposite the market, 9 a day from 0615, 45 mins, US$1.

Long distance The bus station is about 3 km south of the centre. Buses from outside the terminal travel the *Circuito* road. A taxi costs US$2.20. The 2nd-class bus terminal is about 1 km east of the centre along Av Gobernadores, but services are steadily moving to the main terminal. To **Cancún**, 7 daily with **ADO** and **ADO GL**, 7 hrs, US$32-24.50. To **Chetumal**, 1200, 6 hrs, US$42. To **Ciudad del Carmen**, frequent ADO services, 3 hrs, US$11. To **Escárcega**, frequent, 2 hrs, US$7.50. To **Mérida**, frequent **ADO** services, 2½ hrs, US$9.50. To **Mexico City**, ADO at 1230, 2225, 2345, 18 hrs, US$68, and 2 **ADO GL** services at 1430 and 1635, 16 hrs, US$82. To **San Cristóbal de las Casas**, OCC at 2145, 11 hrs, US$25. To **Veracruz**, luxury only, ADO GL at 2215, 11½ hrs, US$52.50. To **Villahermosa**, frequent **ADO** services, 6-7 hrs, US$21.

Car
Car hire Maya Nature, Av Ruiz Cortines 51, inside Hotel del Mar, T981-811 9191. **Hertz** and **Autorent** car rentals at airport.

● Directory

Ciudad del Carmen *p21*
Banks **Banamex**, Calle 24 No 63 or **Banorte**, Calle 30 and 33. **Post** Calle 22 No 136.

Campeche *p24, map p25*
Banks **Banorte**, Calle 8 No 237, between Calle 57 and Calle 59; Mon-Fri 0900-1700; **HSBC**, Calle 10 No 311, Mon-Fri 0900-1700, Sat 0900-1500; **Santander Serfín**, Calle 57 No 8; **American Express**, T981-811 1010, Calle 59, Edificio Belmar, oficina 5, helpful for lost cheques, etc. Plenty of ATMs and places to get cash on credit cards. **Cultural centres** Casa del Teniente de Rey, Calle 59 No 38 between 14 and 16, houses the Instituto Nacional de Antropología e Historia (INAH), dedicated to the restoration of Maya ruins in the state of Campeche, as well as supporting local museums. INAH can be visited for information regarding any of the sites in the state, T981-811 1314, www.inah.gob.mx. The **Centro Cultural Casa 6**, Calle 57, between Calle 8 and 10, 0900-2100 daily, US$0.35, is housed in a handsome building on the main plaza. It conjures the opulence and splendour of Campeche's golden days. **Immigration** The Oficina de Migración is inside the Palacio Federal. **Internet** Many internet places around town, including **Cybercafé Campeche**, Calle 61 between Calle 10 and 12, 0900-1300, US$1.50 per hr. **Laundry** Antigua, Calle 57 between Calle 12 and 14, US$1 per kg. **Medical services** Red Cross, T981-815 2411. **Post** Av 16 de Septiembre (Malecón) and Calle 53 in Edificio Federal; Mon-Fri 0800-2000, Sat 0900-1300 for *Lista de Correos*, registered mail, money orders and stamps. **Telephone** Telmex, Calle 8 between Calle 51 y 53, free; Calle 51 No 45, between Calle 12 and 14.

State of Yucatán

The archaeological sites of Chichén Itzá, Oxkintoc, Uxmal, Kabah and Labná are just a few of the many strewn throughout the State of Yucatán. Try not to miss Dzibilchaltún; the intrusion of European architecture is nowhere more startling than here. The region's many cenotes *(deep pools created by the disintegration of the dry land above an underground river) were sacred to the Maya, who threw precious jewels, silverware and even humans into their depths; many are perfect for swimming. On the coast, boat trips are organized to observe pelicans, egrets and flamingos in their natural habitat. It is possible to visit some of the impressive* henequén *(sisal) haciendas in the more rural areas and admire the showy mansions that line the Paseo de Montejo in Mérida.*

North to Mérida → *For listings, see pages 48-60.*

At **Maxcanú**, the road to Muná and Ticul branches east; a short way down it is the recently restored Maya site of **Oxkintoc** ① *US$3*. The Pyramid of the Labyrinth can be entered (take a torch) and there are other ruins, some with figures. Ask for a guide at the village of Calcehtoc, which is 4 km from the ruins and from the Grutas de Oxkintoc (no bus service). These, however, cannot compare with the caves at Loltún or Balankanché (see pages 40 and 45). Highway 180 continues north towards Mérida through a region of numerous *cenotes*, soon passing a turn-off to the turn-of-the-20th-century Moorish-style *henequén* (sisal) hacienda at **San Bernardo**, one of a number in the state that can be visited; an interesting museum chronicling the old Yucatán Peninsula tramway system is located in its spacious grounds. Running beside the railway, the highway continues 47 km to its junction with the inland route at **Umán**, a *henequén* processing town with another large 17th-century church and convent dedicated to St Francis of Assisi; there are many *cenotes* in the flat surrounding limestone plain. If driving, Highway 180/261 is a divided four-lane motorway for the final 18-km stretch into Mérida. There is a ring road around the city.

Mérida → *For listings, see pages 48-60. Phone code: 999.*

The capital of Yucatán state and its colonial heart, Mérida is a bustling, tightly packed city full of colonial buildings in varying states of repair. There is continual activity in the centre, with a huge influx of tourists during the high season mingling with busy Meridanos going about their daily business. Although the city has been developed over many years for tourism, there is plenty of local flavour for the traveller to seek out off the beaten track. Attempts to create a sophisticated Champs Elysées-style boulevard in the north of the city at Paseo Montejo have not been quite successful; the plan almost seems to go against the grain of Mérida's status as an ancient city, which has gradually evolved into a place with its own distinct identity.

Ins and outs

Getting there All buses from outside Yucatán State arrive at the CAME terminal on Calle 70 between Calle 69 y 71, a few blocks from the centre. There is another bus terminal around the corner on Calle 69, where buses from local destinations such as Uxmal arrive. The airport is 8 km from the city, bus 79 takes you to the centre. Taxis to the centre from the airport charge US$9.

Getting around You can see most of Mérida on foot. Although the city is big, there is not much to concern the tourist outside a few blocks radiating from the main plaza. The VW Beetle taxis are expensive, due to their scarcity; fares start at US$3 for a short journey. *Colectivo* buses are difficult to locate; they appear suddenly on the bigger roads in the city, you can flag them down anywhere. They terminate at the market; flat fare US$0.25.

Tourist information The main **tourist office** ① *Calle 60 y Calle 57 (just off Parque Hidalgo), daily 0800-2000,* is very helpful. There are other tourist offices on the main plaza by the Palacio Municipio and at the airport. You'll find good information online at www.mayayucatan.com.mx and www.yucatantoday.com.

Safety Mérida is a safe city, with its own **tourist police** ① *T999-930 3200,* recognizable by their brown and white uniforms.

Best time to visit During July and August, although very hot, Mérida is subject to heavy rains during the afternoon.

Background

Mérida was originally a large Maya city called Tihoo. It was conquered on 6 January 1542, by Francisco de Montejo. He dismantled the pyramids of the Maya and used the stone as the foundations for the cathedral of San Ildefonso, built 1556-1559. For the next 300 years, Mérida remained under Spanish control, unlike the rest of Mexico, which was governed from the capital. During the Caste Wars of 1847-1855, Mérida held out against the marauding forces of indigenous armies, who had defeated the Mexican army in every other city in the Yucatán Peninsula except Campeche. Reinforcements from the centre allowed the Mexicans to regain control of their city, but the price was to relinquish control of the region to Mexico City.

Sights

The city revolves around the large, shady zócalo, site of the **cathedral**, completed in 1559, the oldest cathedral in Latin America, which has an impressive baroque façade. It contains the Cristo de las Ampollas (Christ of the Blisters), a statue carved from a tree that burned for a whole night after being hit by lightning, without showing any damage at all. Placed in the church at Ichmul, it then suffered only a slight charring (hence the name) when the church was burned to the ground. To the left of the cathedral on the adjacent side of the

Mérida

Sleeping 🛏
Casa Becil **1** D2
Casa Bowen **2** D2
Casa MExilio **10** B1
Casa San Angel **18** A3
Casa San Juan **16** D2
Dolores Alba **4** C4
Gobernador **5** B2
Gran **6** C3
Hacienda Xcanatún **8** A3
Hostal Zócalo **17** C2
La Misión de
 Fray Diego **7** C2
Las Monjas **9** C2

Margarita **11** C2
Medio Mundo **19** B2
Mucuy **12** B3
Nómadas Youth
 Hostal **13** B2
Posada Toledo **14** B3
San José **15** C2
Trailer Park Rainbow **3** A3
Trinidad **22** B2

Eating 🍴
Alberto's Continental **5** B2
Amaro **1** B2
Café Alameda **16** B3

Café Chocolate **23** B3
Café El Hoyo **15** B2
Café La Habana **8** B2
Café Petropolis **2** D2
Colonial **12** B2
El Colón Sorbetes y
 Dulces Finos **10** C3
El Nuevo Tucho **4** B3
El Trapiche **3** C2
Flor de Santiago **14** B1
Italian Coffee
 Company **9** C2
Jugos California **6** C2
La Casa de Frida **24** C2

La Vía Olympo **11** C2
Los Almendros **7** B4
Marlín Azul **18** B2
Marys **21** C3
Mérida **20** C2
Pórtico del Peregrino **17** B2
Villa Maria **13** B1
Vito Corleone's Pizza **19** B2

Bars & clubs 🎵
La Parranda **22** C3
Panchos **12** B2

plaza is the **Palacio de Gobierno**, built 1892. It houses a collection of enormous murals by Fernando Castro Pacheco, depicting the struggle of the Maya to integrate with the Spanish. The murals can be viewed until 2000 every day. **Casa de Montejo** is on the south side of the plaza, a 16th-century palace built by the city's founder, now a branch of Banamex. Away from the main Plaza along Calle 60 is Parque Hidalgo, a charming tree-filled square, which borders the 17th-century **Iglesia de Jesús**. A little further along Calle 60 is the **Teatro Peón Contreras**, built at the beginning of the 20th century by an Italian architect, with a neoclassical façade, marble staircase and Italian frescoes.

There are several 16th- and 17th-century churches dotted about the city: **La Mejorada**, behind the Museum of Peninsular Culture (Calle 59 between 48 and 50), **Tercera Orden**, **San Francisco** and **San Cristóbal** (beautiful, in the centre). The **Ermita**, an 18th-century chapel with beautiful grounds, is a lonely, deserted place 10 to 15 minutes from the centre.

Museo de Antropología e Historia ① *Paseo de Montejo 485, Tue-Sat 0800-2000, Sun 0800-1400, US$3.70*, housed in the beautiful neoclassical Palacio Cantón, has an excellent collection of original Maya artefacts from various sites in the Yucatán state. The displays are very well laid out, and the explanations are all in Spanish. There are many examples of jade jewellery dredged from *cenotes*, and some examples of cosmetically deformed skulls with sharpened teeth. This is a good overview of the history of the Maya.

Museo Macay ① *Calle 60, on the main plaza, www.macay.org, daily 1000-1730, free*, has a permanent exhibition of Yucatecan artists, with temporary exhibits by contemporary local artists. **Museo de Arte Popular** ① *Calle 59 esq 50, Barrio de la Mejorada, Tue-Sat 0900-2000, Sun 0800-1400, free*, has a permanent exhibition of Maya art, handicrafts and clothing, with a good souvenir shop attached. **Museo de la Canción Yucateca** ① *Calle 57 between 50 and 48, www.merida.gob.mx/historia/lugaresmuseocancion.html, Tue-Sun 0900-1700, US$1.50*, in the Casa de la Cultura, has an exhibition of objects and instruments relating to the history of music in the region. **Pinacoteca Juan Gamboa Guzmán** ① *Calle 59 , Tue-Sat 0800-2000, Sun 0800-1400, free*, is a gallery showing old and contemporary painting and sculpture. Fans of John Lloyd Steven's seminal travelogue *Incidents of Travel in Central America, Chiapas and Yucatán* should check out **Casa Catherwood** ① *Calle 59 between 72 and 74, daily 0900-1400 and 1700-2100, US$5*. Dedicated to Steven's companion and illustrator, Mr Catherwood, this museum contains stunning colour lithographs of Mayan ruins, as they were found in the 19th century.

Around Mérida → *For listings, see pages 48-60.*

Celestún → *Phone code: 988.*

A small, dusty fishing resort west of Mérida much frequented in summer by Mexicans, Celestún stands on the spit of land separating the Río Esperanza estuary from the ocean. The long beach is relatively clean except near the town proper, with clear water ideal for swimming, although rising afternoon winds usually churn up silt and there is little shade; along the beach are many fishing boats bristling with *jimbas* (cane poles), used for catching local octopus. There are beach restaurants with showers. A plain zócalo watched over by a simple stucco church is the centre for what little happens in town. Cafés (some with hammock space for rent) spill onto the sand, from which parents watch offspring splash in the surf. Even the unmarked **post office** ① *Mon-Fri 0900-1300*, is a private residence the rest of the week.

Know your hammock

Different materials are available for hammocks. Some you might find include **sisal**, which is very strong, light, hard-wearing but rather scratchy and uncomfortable, and is identified by its distinctive smell; **cotton**, which is soft, flexible, comfortable, not as hard-wearing but, with care, is good for four or five years of everyday use. It is not possible to weave cotton and sisal together, although you may be told otherwise, so mixtures are unavailable. **Cotton/silk** mixtures are offered, but will probably be an artificial silk. **Nylon** is very strong and light but it's hot in hot weather and cold in cold weather.

Never buy your first hammock from a street vendor and never accept a packaged hammock without checking the size and quality. The surest way to judge a good hammock is by weight: 1.5 kg (3.3 lb) is a fine item, under 1 kg (2.2 lb) is junk (advises Alan Handleman, a US expert). Also, the finer and thinner the strands of material, the more strands there will be, and the more comfortable the hammock. The best hammocks are the so-called 3-ply, but they are difficult to find. There are three sizes: single (sometimes called doble), matrimonial and family (buy a matrimonial at least for comfort). If judging by end-strings, 50 would be sufficient for a child, 150 would suit a medium-sized adult, 250 a couple. Prices vary considerably so shop around and bargain hard.

The immediate region is a biosphere reserve, created to protect the thousands of migratory waterfowl who inhabit the lagoons; fish, crabs and shrimp also spawn here, and kingfishers, black hawks, wood storks and crocodiles may sometimes be glimpsed in the quieter waterways. In the winter months Celestún plays host to the largest flamingo colony in North America, perhaps more than 20,000 birds – in the summer most of the flamingos leave Celestún for their nesting grounds in the Río Lagartos area. Boat trips to view the wildlife can be arranged at the **visitor centre** ① *below the river bridge 1 km back along the Mérida road* (US$60 for one six people, plus US$4 per person for the reserve entrance fees, 1½ hours). Make sure your boatman takes you through the mangrove channel and to the Baldiosera freshwater spring in addition to visiting the flamingos. It is often possible to see flamingos from the bridge early in the morning and the road to it may be alive with egrets, herons and pelicans. January to March is the best time to see them. It's important to wear a hat and use sunscreen. There are hourly buses to Mérida's terminal at Calle 50 and 67, 0530-2000, two hours, US$4.

Progreso and around → *Phone code: 969.*

Thirty-six kilometres north of Mérida, Progreso has the nearest beach to the city. It is a slow-growing resort town, with the facilities improving to service the increasing number of US cruise ships that arrive every Wednesday. Progreso is famous for its industrial pier, which at 6 km is the longest in the world. It has been closed to the public since someone fell off the end on a moped. The beach is long and clean and the water is shallow and good for swimming.

A short bus journey (4 km) west from Progreso are **Puerto Yucalpetén** and **Chelem**. Balneario Yucalpetén has a beach with lovely shells, but also a large naval base with further construction in progress.

Five kilometres east of Progreso is another resort, **Chicxulub**; it has a narrow beach, quiet and peaceful, on which are many boats and much seaweed. Small restaurants sell fried fish by the *ración*, or kilogram, served with tortillas, mild chilli and *cebolla curtida* (pickled onion). Chicxulub is reputed to be the site of the crater made by a meteorite crash 65 million years ago, which caused the extinction of the dinosaurs. (The site is actually offshore on the ocean floor.) The beaches on this coast are often deserted and, between December and February, 'El Norte' wind blows in every 10 days or so, making the water turbid and bringing in cold, rainy weather.

Dzibilchaltún
ⓘ *0800-1700, US$5.80.*
Halfway between Mérida and Progreso turn right for the Maya ruins of Dzibilchaltún. This unique city, according to carbon dating, was founded as early as 1000 BC. The site is in two halves, connected by a *sacbé* (sacred road). The most important building is the **Templo de Las Siete Muñecas** (Temple of the Seven Dolls), at the east end, which is partly restored. At the west end is the ceremonial centre with temples, houses and a large plaza in which the open chapel, simple and austere, sticks out like a sore thumb. The evangelizing friars had clearly hijacked a pre-Conquest sacred area in which to erect a symbol of the invading religion. At its edge is the **Cenote Xlaca** containing very clear water that is 44 m deep (you can swim in it, take mask and snorkel as it is full of fascinating fish); there's a very interesting nature trail starting halfway between the temple and the *cenote*; the trail rejoins the *sacbé* halfway along. The **museum** is at the entrance by the ticket office (site map available). *Combis* stop here en route to **Chablekal**, a village along the same road.

The Convent Route → *For listings, see pages 48-60.*

The route takes in Maya villages and ruins, colonial churches, cathedrals, convents and *cenotes*. It is best to be on the road by 0800 with a full gas tank. Get on the Periférico to Ruta 18 (signs say Kanasín, not Ruta 18). At **Kanasín**, La Susana is known especially for local delicacies like *sopa de lima*, *salbutes* and *panuchos*. Clean, excellent service and abundant helpings at reasonable prices. Follow the signs to **Acanceh**. Here you will see the unusual combination of the Grand Pyramid, a colonial church and a modern church, all on the same small plaza (similar to the Plaza de las Tres Culturas in Tlatelolco, Mexico City). About four blocks away is the Temple of the Stuccoes, with hieroglyphs. Eight kilometres further south is **Tecoh**, with an ornate church and convent dedicated to the Virgin of the Assumption. There are some impressive carved stones around the altar. The church and convent both stand at the base of a large Maya pyramid. Nearby are the caverns of **Dzab-Náh**; you must take a guide as there are treacherous drops into *cenotes*. Next on the route is **Telchaquillo**, a small village with an austere chapel and a beautiful *cenote* in the plaza, with carved steps for easy access.

Mayapán and around
ⓘ *US$2.40.*
A few kilometres off the main road to the right you will find the Maya ruins of Mayapán, a walled city with 4000 mounds, six of which are in varying stages of restoration. Mayapán, along with Uxmal and Chichén Itzá, once formed a triple alliance, and the site is as big as

Chichén Itzá, with some buildings being replicas of those at the latter site. The restoration process is ongoing; the archaeologists can be watched as they unearth more and more buildings of this large, peaceful, late-Maya site. Mayapán is easily visited by bus from Mérida (every 30 minutes from terminal at Calle 50 y 67 behind the municipal market, one hour, US$1 to Telchaquillo). It can also be reached from Oxcutzcab.

Thirty kilometres along the main road is **Tekit**, a large village containing the church of San Antonio de Padua, with many ornate statues of saints. The next village, 7 km further on, is called **Mama**, with the oldest church on the route, famous for its ornate altar and bell-domed roof. Another 9 km is **Chumayel**, where the legendary Maya document *Chilam Balam* was found. Four kilometres ahead is **Teabo**, with an impressive 17th-century church. Next comes **Tipikal**, a small village with an austere church.

Maní

Twelve kilometres further on is Maní, the most important stop on this route. Here you will find a large church, convent and museum with explanations in English, Spanish and one of the Maya languages. It was here that Fray Diego de Landa ordered important Maya documents and artefacts to be burned, during an intense period of Franciscan conversion of the Maya people to Christianity. When Diego realized his great error, he set about trying to write down all he could remember of the 27 scrolls and hieroglyphs he had destroyed, along with 5000 idols, 13 altars and 127 vases. The text, entitled *Relation of Things in Yucatán*, is still available today, unlike the artefacts. To return to Mérida, head for Ticul, to the west, then follow the main road via Muná.

Ticul and Oxkutzcab → *Phone code: 997.*

Eighty kilometres south of Mérida, Ticul is a small, pleasant little village known for its *huípiles*, the embroidered white dresses worn by the older Maya women. You can buy them in the tourist shops in Mérida, but the prices and quality of the ones in Ticul will be much better. It is also a good base for visiting smaller sites in the south of Yucatán state, such as Sayil, Kabah, Xlapak and Labná (see below).

Sixteen kilometres southeast of Ticul is Oxkutzcab, a good centre for catching buses to Chetumal, Muná, Mayapán and Mérida (US$2.20). It's a friendly place with a market by the plaza and a church with a 'two-dimensional' façade on the other side of the square.

Grutas de Loltún and around

ⓘ *Tue-Sun 0930, 1100, 1230 and 1400. US$3 with obligatory guide, 1 hr 20 mins. Recommended. Caretaker may admit tours on Mon, but there is no lighting.*

Nearby, to the south, are the caverns and pre-Columbian vestiges at Loltún (supposedly extending for 8 km). Take a pickup (US$0.30) or truck from the market going to Cooperativa (an agricultural town). For return, flag down a passing truck. Alternatively, take a taxi, US$10 (can be visited from Labná on a tour from Mérida). The area around Ticul and Oxkutzcab is intensively farmed with citrus fruits, papayas and mangoes. After Oxkutzcab on Route 184 is **Tekax** with restaurant **La Ermita** serving excellent Yucatecan dishes at reasonable prices. From Tekax a paved road leads to the ruins of **Chacmultún**. From the top you have a beautiful view. There is a caretaker. All the towns between Muná and Peto, 14 km northeast of Oxkutzcab off Route 184, have large old churches. Beyond the Peto turn-off the scenery is scrub and swamp as far as the Belizean border.

The Puuc Route

Taking in the four sites of Kabah, Sayil, Xlapak and Labná, as well as Uxmal, this journey explores the hilly (or *puuc* in Maya) region to the south of Mérida. All five sites can be visited in a day on the 'Ruta Puuc' bus, which departs from the first-class bus station in Mérida every day at 0800, US$11, entry to sites not included. This is a good whistle-stop tour, but does not give you much time at each of the ruins, but five sites in one day is normally enough for most enthusiasts; if you want to spend longer seeing these sites, stay overnight in Ticul.

Kabah
① *0800-1700, US$3.*
On either side of the main road, 37 km south of Uxmal and often included in tours of the latter, are the ruins of Kabah. On one side there is a fascinating **Palace of Masks** (*Codz-Poop*), whose façade bears the image of Chac, mesmerically repeated 260 times, the number of days in the Almanac Year. Each mask is made up of 30 units of mosaic stone. Even the central chamber is entered via a huge Chac mask whose curling snout forms the doorstep. On the other side of this wall, beneath the figure of the ruler, Kabal, are impressive carvings on the door arches, which depict a man about to be killed, pleading for mercy, and two men duelling. This side of the road is mostly reconstructed; across the road the outstanding feature is a reconstructed arch marking the start of the *sacbé* (sacred road), which leads all the way to Uxmal, and several stabilized, but impossible to climb mounds of collapsed buildings being renovated. The style is Classic Puuc.

Sayil, Xlapak and Labná
① *Entrance US$3 at each site.*
Sayil means 'The Place of the Ants'. Dating from AD 800-1000, this site has an interesting palace, which in its day included 90 bathrooms for some 350 people. The simple, elegant colonnade is reminiscent of the architecture of ancient Greece. The central motif on the upper part of the façade is a broad mask with huge fangs, flanked by two serpents surrounding the grotesque figure of a descending deity. From the upper level of the palace you can see a tiny ruin on the side of a mountain called the Nine Masks.

Thirteen kilometres from Sayil, the ruins of **Xlapak** have not been as extensively restored as the others in this region. There are 14 mounds and three partially restored pyramids.

Labná has a feature that ranks it among the most outstanding sites of the Puuc region: a monumental arch connecting two groups of buildings (now in ruins), which displays an architectural concept unique to this region. Most Maya arches are purely structural, but the one at Labná has been constructed for aesthetic purposes, running right through the façade and clearly meant to be seen from afar. The two façades on either side of the arch differ greatly; the one at the entrance is beautifully decorated with delicate latticework and stone carving imitating the wood or palm-frond roofs of Maya huts.

Uxmal → *For listings, see pages 48-60. Phone code: 997.*

ⓘ *Daily 0800-1700, US$9.50 including light and sound show; rental of translation equipment US$2.50. Shows are at 2000 in summer and 1900 in winter. Mixed reports. Guides available with 1½-hr tours. Tours in Spanish US$40, in English, French, German and Italian US$45. For transport to Uxmal, see page 58.*

Built during the Classic period, Uxmal is the most famous of the ruins in the Puuc region. The characteristic features of Maya cities in this region are the quadrangular layout of the buildings, set on raised platforms, and an artificially created underground water-storage system. The **Pyramid of the Sorcerer** is an unusual oval-shaped pyramid set on a large rectangular base; there is evidence that five stages of building were used in its construction. The pyramid is 30 m tall, with two temples at the top. The **Nunnery** is set around a large courtyard, with some fine masks of Chac, the rain god, on the corners of the buildings. The east building of the Nunnery is decorated with double-headed serpents on its cornices. There are some plumed serpents in relief, in excellent condition, on the façade of the west building. The **House of the Governor** is 100 m long, and is considered one of the most outstanding buildings in all of Mesoamerica. Two arched passages divide the building into three distinct sections that would probably have been covered over. Above the central entrance is an elaborate trapezoidal motif, with a string of Chaac masks interwoven into a flowing, undulating serpent-like shape extending to the façade's two corners. The stately two-headed jaguar throne in front of the structure suggests a royal or administrative function. The **House of the Turtles** is sober by comparison, its simple walls adorned with carved turtles on the upper cornice, above a short row of tightly packed columns, which resemble the Maya *palapas*, made of sticks with a thatched roof, still used today. The **House of the Doves** is the oldest and most damaged of the buildings at Uxmal. It is still impressive: a long, low platform of wide columns topped by clusters of roof combs, whose similarity to dovecotes gave the building its name.

Izamal and around → *For listings, see pages 48-60. Phone code: 988.*

Sixty-eight kilometres east of Mérida is the friendly little town of Izamal. Once a major Classic Maya religious site founded by the priest Itzamná, Izamal became one of the centres of the Spanish attempt to Christianize the Maya.

Fray Diego de Landa, the historian of the Spanish conquest of Mérida (of whom there is a statue in the town), founded the huge **convent** and **church**, which now face the main **Plaza de la Constitución**. This building, constructed on top of a Maya pyramid, was begun in 1549 and has the second largest atrium in the world. If you carefully examine the walls that surround the magnificent atrium, you will notice that some of the faced stones are embellished with carvings of Maya origin, confirming that, when they had toppled the pre-Columbian structures, the Spaniards re-used the material to create the imported architecture. There is also a throne built for the Pope's visit in 1993. The image of the Inmaculada Virgen de la Concepción in the magnificent church was made the Reina de Yucatán in 1949, and the patron saint of the state in 1970. Just 2½ blocks away, visible from the convent across a second square and signposted, are the ruins of a great mausoleum known as the **Kinich-Kakmo pyramid** ⓘ *0800-1700, free, entrance next to the tortilla factory.* You climb the first set of stairs to a broad, tree-covered platform, at the end of which is a further pyramid (still under reconstruction). From the top there is an excellent view of the town and surrounding *henequén* and citrus plantations. Kinich-Kakmo is 195 m long, 173 m wide and 36 m high, the fifth highest in Mexico. In all, 20 Maya structures have been identified in Izamal, several on Calle 27. Another startling feature about the town is that the entire colonial centre, including the convent, the arcaded government offices on Plaza de la Constitución and the arcaded second square, is painted a rich yellow ochre, giving it the nickname of the 'golden city'.

From Izamal you can go by bus to **Cenotillo**, where there are several fine *cenotes* within easy walking distance from the town (avoid the one *in* town), especially **Ucil**, excellent for swimming, and **La Unión**. Take the same bus as for Izamal from Mérida. Past Cenotillo is Espita and then a road forks left to Tizimín (see page 47).

The cemetery of **Hoctún**, on the Mérida-Chichén road, is also worth visiting; indeed it is impossible to miss, there is an 'Empire State Building' on the site. Take a bus from Mérida (last bus back 1700) to see extensive ruins at **Aké**, an unusual structure. Public transport in Mérida is difficult: from an unsigned stop on the corner of Calle 53 y 50, some buses to Tixkokob and Ekmul continue to Aké; ask the driver.

Chichén Itzá → *For listings, see pages 48-60.*

ⓘ *Daily 0800-1730, US$9.50 including light and sound show, free bag storage, free for Mexicans on Sun and holidays, when it is incredibly crowded; you may leave and re-enter as often as you like on day of issue. Guided tours US$40 per group of any size; it is best to try and join one, many languages available. Best to arrive before 1030 to beat the crowds. The tourist centre at the entrance to the ruins has a restaurant and small museum, bookshop and souvenir shop with exchange facilities. Drinks, snacks and toilets are available at the entrance and at the cenote. Take a hat, suncream, sunglasses, shoes with good grip and drinking water.*

Chichén Itzá means 'mouth of the well of the water-sorcerer' and is one of the most spectacular of Maya sites. The Castillo, a giant stepped pyramid dominates the site, watched over by Chacmool, a Maya fertility god who reclines on a nearby structure. The city was built by the Maya in late Classic times (AD 600-900). By the end of the 10th century, the city was more or less abandoned. It was re-established in the 11th to 12th centuries, but much debate surrounds by whom. Whoever the people were, a comparison of some of the architecture with that of Tula, north of Mexico City, indicates they were heavily influenced by the Toltecs of Central Mexico.

The major buildings in the north half display a Toltec influence. Dominating them is **El Castillo** ⓘ *1100-1500, 1600-1700, closed if raining*, its top decorated by the symbol of Quetzalcoatl/Kukulcán, the plumed serpent god. The balustrade of the 91 stairs up each of the four sides is also decorated at its base by the head of a plumed, open-mouthed serpent. The interior ascent of 61 steep and narrow steps leading to a chamber is currently closed; the red-painted jaguar that probably served as the throne of the high priest once burned bright, its eyes of jade, its fangs of flint.

There is a **ball court** with grandstand and towering walls, each set with a projecting ring of stone high up; at eye-level is a relief showing the decapitation of the winning captain (sacrifice was an honour; some theories, however, maintain that it was the losing captain who was killed). El Castillo stands at the centre of the northern half of the site, and almost at a right angle to its northern face runs the *sacbé* (sacred road), to the **Cenote**

Chichén Itzá

Main Entrance

North Half

South Half

OLD CHICHEN

Entrance from Hotels

N

100 metres
100 yards

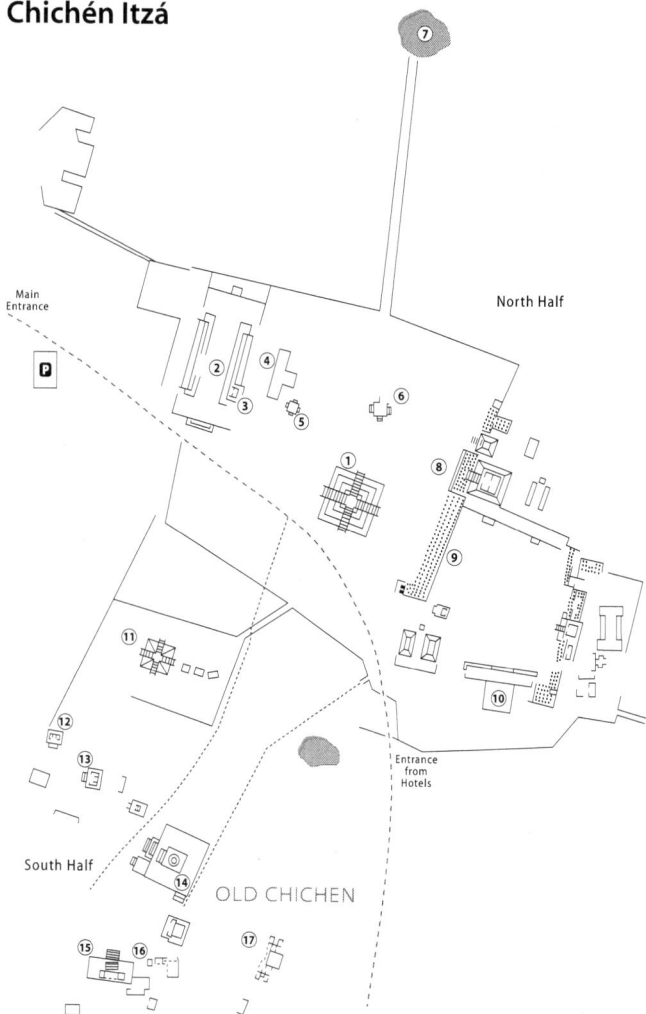

El Castillo **1**
Ball Court **2**
Temple of the Jaguar **3**
Platform of the Skulls
  (Tzompantli) **4**
Platform of Eagles **5**
Platform of Venus **6**

Cenote Sagrado (Well of
  Sacrifice) **7**
Temple of the Warriors
  & Chacmool Statue **8**
Group of a Thousand
  Columns **9**
Market **10**
Tomb of the High Priest **11**

House of the Deer **12**
Red House **13**
El Caracol (Observatory) **14**
Casa de las Monjas
  (Nunnery) **15**
'Church' **16**
Akabdzilo **17**

Sagrado (Well of Sacrifice). Into the Cenote Sagrado were thrown valuable propitiatory objects of all kinds, animals and human sacrifices. The well was first dredged by Edward H Thompson, the US Consul in Mérida, between 1904 and 1907; he accumulated a vast quantity of objects in pottery, jade, copper and gold. In 1962 the well was explored again by an expedition sponsored by the National Geographic Society and some 4000 further artefacts were recovered, including beads, polished jade, lumps of *copal* resin, small bells, a statuette of rubber latex, another of wood, and a quantity of animal and human bones. Another *cenote*, the Cenote Xtoloc, was probably used as a water supply. To the east of El Castillo is the **Templo de los Guerreros** (Temple of the Warriors) with its famous reclining **Chacmool** statue. This pyramidal platform is closed off to avoid erosion.

Chichén Viejo (Old Chichén), where the Maya buildings of the earlier city are found, lies about 500 m by path from the main clearing. The famous **El Caracol**, or Observatory, is included in this group, as is the **Casa de las Monjas** (Nunnery). A footpath to the right of the Casa de las Monjas leads to the **Templo de los Tres Dinteles** (Temple of the Three Lintels) after 30 minutes' walking. It requires at least one day to see the many pyramids, temples, ball courts and palaces, all of them adorned with astonishing sculptures. Excavation and renovation is still going on. Interesting birdlife and iguanas can also be seen around the ruins.

Note On the morning and afternoon of the spring and autumn equinoxes, the alignment of the sun's shadow casts a serpentine image on the side of the steps of El Castillo.

Grutas de Balankanché
ⓘ *0900-1700, US$5 (allow about 45 mins for the 300-m descent), closed Sat afternoons. The caretaker turns lights on and off, answers questions in Spanish, every hour on the hour, minimum 6, maximum 20 persons.*
Tours run daily to the Grutas de Balankanché caves, 3 km east of Chichén Itzá just off the highway. There are archaeological objects, including offerings of pots and *metates* in an extraordinary setting, except for the unavoidable, awful *son et lumière* show (five a day in Spanish; 1100, 1300 and 1500 in English; 1000 in French; it is very damp and hot, so dress accordingly). To get there, take the Chichén Itzá or Pisté-Balankanché bus hourly at a quarter past, US$0.50, taxi US$15.

Valladolid and around → *For listings, see pages 48-60. Phone code: 985.*

Situated roughly halfway between Mérida and Cancún, Valladolid is a pleasant little town, until now untouched by tourism. Its proximity to the famous ruins of Chichén Itzá, however, means that Valladolid has been earmarked for extensive development by the Mexican government.

Valladolid is set around a large plaza, flanked by the imposing Franciscan cathedral. Most of the hotels are clustered around the centre, as well as numerous restaurants catering for all budgets, favouring the lower end. There is a slightly medieval feel to the city, with some of the streets tapering off into mud tracks. The Vallisoletanos, as they are known, are friendlier than their Meridano neighbours, and Valladolid's location makes it an ideal place to settle for a few days, while exploring the ruins of Chichén Itzá, the fishing village of Río Lagartos on the north coast, and the three beautiful *cenotes* in the area, one of which is right in the town itself, on Calle 36 y 39.

The **tourist office** ① *southeast corner of the plaza*, is not very helpful but they give a useful map. Much more helpful information can be obtained from **Antonio 'Negro' Aguilar** ① *Calle 44 No 195*. Something of a local celebrity, he was a baseball champion in the 1950s and 60s, playing for Mexican squad, the Leones de Yucatán as well as the US team, the Washington Senators. Now he runs a shop selling sports equipment, rents bicycles and rents very cheap accommodation (see Sleeping, page 51). He is glad to offer information on any of the tourist attractions in the area; if cycling around, he will personally draw you a map of the best route you should take. Antonio can also help organize tours in a minivan to the ruins at Ek-Balam, minimum four people, US$3 per person.

Cenote Zací ① *Calle 36 between Calle 37 and 39, daily 0800-1800, US$2, half price for children*, right in town, is an artificially lit *cenote* where you can swim, except when it is occasionally prohibited due to algae in the water. There is a thatched-roof restaurant and lighted promenades. A small town **museum** ① *Calle 41, free*, housed in Santa Ana church, shows the history of rural Yucatán and has some exhibits from recent excavations at the ruins of Ek-Balam.

Seven kilometres from Valladolid is the beautiful **Cenote X-Kekén** ① *daily 0800-1800, US$2.50*, at **Dzitnup**, the name by which it is more commonly known. It is stunningly lit with electric lights, the only natural light source being a tiny hole in the cavernous ceiling dripping with stalactites. Swimming is excellent, the water is cool and refreshing, although reported to be a little dirty, and harmless bats zip around overhead. Exploratory walks can also be made through the many tunnels leading off the *cenote*, for which you will need a torch. *Colectivos* leave when full from in front of **Hotel María Guadalupe**, US$1, they return until 1800, after which you will have to get a taxi back to Valladolid, US$4. Alternatively, hire a bicycle from Antonio Aguilar (see above) and cycle there, 25 minutes. Antonio will explain the best route before you set off. There is also the easily reached *cenote* close by, called **Samulá** ① *US$2.25*, only recently opened to the public.

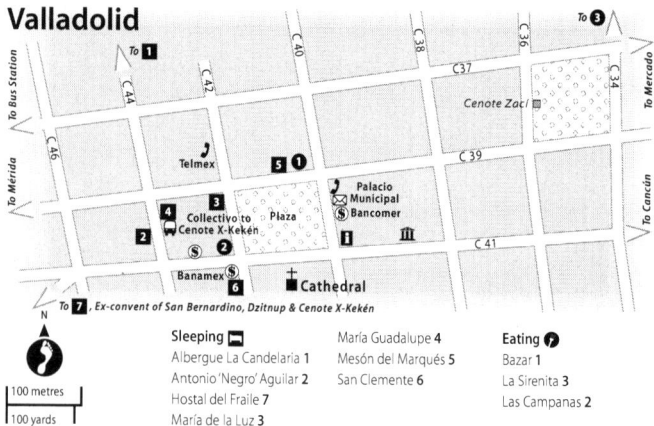

Valladolid

Sleeping 🛏
Albergue La Candelaria 1
Antonio 'Negro' Aguilar 2
Hostal del Fraile 7
María de la Luz 3

María Guadalupe 4
Mesón del Marqués 5
San Clemente 6

Eating 🍴
Bazar 1
La Sirenita 3
Las Campanas 2

Ek-Balam
ⓘ *Daily 0800-1700, US$2.50.*
Twenty-five kilometres north of Valladolid are the Maya ruins of Ek-Balam, meaning 'Black Jaguar'. The ruins contain an impressive series of temples, sacrificial altars and residential buildings grouped around a large central plaza. The main temple, known as 'The Tower', is an immaculate seven-tiered staircase leading up to a flattened area with the remains of a temple. The views are stunning, and because they are not on the tourist trail, these ruins can be viewed at leisure, without the presence of hordes of tour groups from Cancún. To get there by car, take Route 295 north out of Valladolid. Just after the village of Temozón, take the turning on the right for Santa Rita. The ruins are some 5 km further on. A recommended way for those without a car is to hire a bike, take it on the roof of a *colectivo* leaving for Temozón from outside the **Hotel María Guadalupe**, and ask to be dropped off at the turning for Ek-Balam. From there, cycle the remaining 12 km to the ruins. There are also minivans to Ek-Balam run by Antonio Aguilar (see above).

Río Lagartos and around
Tizimín is a dirty, scruffy little town en route to Río Lagartos, where you will have to change buses. If stuck, there are several cheap *posadas* and restaurants, but with frequent buses to Río Lagartos, there should be no need to stay the night here.

Río Lagartos is an attractive little fishing village on the north coast of Yucatán state, whose main attraction is the massive biosphere reserve containing thousands of pink flamingos, as well as 250 other species of bird. The people of Río Lagartos are extremely friendly and very welcoming to tourists. The only route is on the paved road from Valladolid; access from Cancún is by boat only, a journey mainly made by tradesmen ferrying fish to the resort. Development in Río Lagartos, however, is on the horizon.

Boat trips to see the flamingo reserve can be easily arranged by walking down to the harbour and taking your pick from the many offers you'll receive from boatmen. You will get a longer trip with fewer people, due to the decreased weight in the boat. As well as flamingos, there are 250 other species of bird, some very rare, in the 47-sq-km reserve. Make sure your boatman takes you to the larger colony of flamingos near **Las Coloradas** (15 km), recognizable by a large salt mound on the horizon, rather than the smaller groups of birds along the river. Early morning boat trips can be arranged in Río Lagartos to see the flamingos (US$35, in eight to nine seater, 2½ to four hours, cheaper in a five-seater, fix the price before embarking; in mid-week few people go so there is no chance of negotiating, but boat owners are more flexible on where they go; at weekends it is very busy, so it may be easier to get a party together and reduce costs). Check before going whether the flamingos are there; they usually nest here during May and June and stay through July and August (although salt mining is disturbing their habitat).

State of Yucatán listings

For Sleeping and Eating price codes and other relevant information, see pages 12-13.

◆ Sleeping

Mérida *p34, map p36*

The prices of hotels are not determined by their location with budget hotels close to the plaza and the better hotels often further away. If booking into a central hotel, always try to get a room away from the street side, as noise on the narrow streets begins as early as 0500.

$$$$ Hacienda Xcanatún, Km 12 Carretera Mérida–Progreso, T999-941 0273, www.xcanatun.com. Carefully restored hacienda, 10 mins out of town, relaxed atmosphere, full breakfast included, restaurant, **Casa de Piedra**, possibly the best in Mérida, located in a converted machine room with ceilings high enough to give you vertigo, live music Thu, Fri and Sat. Highly recommended.

$$$$-$$$ Casa San Angel, Paseo de Montejo 1 with Calle 49, T999-928 1800, www.hotelcasasanangel.com. A colonial building with gorgeous, high-ceilinged rooms on the ground floor and more rooms upstairs. Quiet, tranquil relaxation pool, restaurant and craft shop. Pleasant.

$$$ Casa Mexilio, Calle 68, between Calle 59 and 57, T999-928 2505, casamexilio@ earthlink.net. This fabulous, old-fashioned colonial building has 3 floors complete with antique sitting room, lush courtyard and a pleasant pool. Part of a bygone world and a soothing place to stay. Breakfast included. Friendly hosts. Recommended.

$$$ Gobernador, Calle 59 No 535, corner of 66, T999-930 4141, www.gobernador merida.com.mx. Good clean hotel with 2 small pools. All rooms with a/c, cable TV and phone. 'Executive' rooms are better. Restaurant offers buffet breakfast. Promotional rates and free Wi-Fi. Recommended.

$$$ La Misión de Fray Diego, Calle 61 No 524 between Calle 64 and 66, T01-800-221-0599, www.lamisiondefraydiego.com. Very pleasant colonial-style hotel situated around 2 shady courtyards. Section nearest the road is original 17th century, formerly connected to the convent behind. Minibar and TV in all rooms, small pool and restaurant.

$$$-$$ Gran Hotel, Parque Hidalgo, Calle 60 No 496, esq Calle 59, T999-923 6963, www.granhoteldemerida.com.mx. A great place to stay with a good atmosphere. Popular with the stars of film and stage, and politicians, including Fidel Castro. All rooms are clean and have a/c, TV, hot water and phone; not all have windows. Free parking.

$$$-$$ Medio Mundo, Calle 55 No 533 between Calle 64 and 66, T999-924 5472, www.hotelmediomundo.com. Renovated old home now a charming hotel with 12 tasteful, high-ceiling rooms, lush garden patio and swimming pool. Friendly, pleasant and quaint. Nice handicraft shop forms part of the hotel. Recommended.

$$ Casa San Juan, Calle 62 No 545A between Calle 69 and 71, T999-986 2937, www.casasanjuan.com. This restored 19th-century house, close to the bus station, has a pleasant, tranquil atmosphere. The multilingual owner is helpful and friendly,the rooms are large, and prices include American breakfast. Book ahead in high season.

$$ Dolores Alba Mérida, Calle 63 No 464 between Calle 52 and 54, T999-858 1555, www.doloresalba.com. This large, modern hotel has 2 sections and price bands. The more comfortable and expensive rooms overlook the pool and courtyard. The cheaper rooms are slightly smaller and have no views. Cool, airy atmosphere and a nice pool. All rooms have a/c, and there's a sister establishment in Chichén Itzá.

$$ Posada Toledo, Calle 58 No 487 esq 57, T999-923 1690, hptoledo@prodigy.net.mx.

This charming old hotel has a strong, if slightly tired, character. Elegant, high-ceiling rooms surround a plant-filled courtyard, all adorned with interesting woodwork and occasionally weathered, antique furniture. Cheap breakfast, parking (US$4) and colour TV.

$$-$ Trinidad, Calle 62 No 464 esq 55, T999-923 2033, www.hotelestrinidad.com. This old house, popular with budget travellers and backpackers, has a relaxed, friendly vibe. Pool table, DVDs, courtyard and rooftop jacuzzi – the perfect way to unwind after a hard day pounding the streets. Continental breakfast included in the price. Simply lovely and highly recommended.

$ Casa Becil, Calle 67 No 550-C, between Calle 66 and 68, T999-924 6764, hotelcasa becil@yahoo.com.mx. The rooms are bright and clean, if simple. They all have fan, bath, hot water and cable TV. The owner is English speaking and hospitable. There's also a communal kitchen. Conveniently located for the bus station. Recommended.

$ Casa Bowen, corner of Calle 66 No 521-B, esq 65, T999-928 6109. Open 24 hrs, if locked ring bell. Restored colonial house, the staff are friendly and English speaking, and rooms have bath and hot water, cheaper with fan. Often full at weekends. Avoid rooms overlooking the main street – they're noisy. Nicely located between the CAME 1st-class bus terminal and the centre.

$ Hostal Zócalo, on the south of the plaza, T999-930 9562, hostel_zocalo@yahoo.com. Popular hostel with economical rooms and big, clean dormitories. There's TV, DVD, kitchen, laundry and internet. Full breakfast included with the private rooms. Friendly management and good location.

$ Las Monjas, Calle 66A No 509 between Calle 61 and 63, T999-928 6632. Simple, family-run lodgings. Clean, quiet, friendly and good value. Can organize tours. Recommended.

$ Margarita, Calle 66 No 506 and 63, T999-923 7236. With shower, clean, good, rooms a

bit dark and noisy downstairs, cheaper rooms for 5 (3 beds), parking, friendly, excellent value. Some rooms have TV and a/c (pricier).

$ Mucuy, Calle 57 No 481, between Calle 56 and 58, T999-928 5193, www.mucuy.com. Good, but 1st-floor rooms are very hot. There's a pool and garden, hot water and optional TV. Run by a lovely English-speaking, elderly woman and her daughter. Highly recommended.

$ Nómadas Youth Hostal, Calle 62 No 433, end of Calle 51, 5 blocks north of the plaza, T999-924 5223, www.nomadas travel.com. A clean and friendly hostel with private rooms and dorms. General services include hot water, full kitchen, drinking water, hammocks, swimming pool and internet. Owner Raúl speaks English and is very helpful. Good value and a great place to meet other travellers. Free salsa classes every night. Live 'trova' music Mon, Wed. Fri. Recommended.

$ San José, west of plaza on Calle 63 No 503, between Calle 64 and 66, T999-928 6657, san_jose92@latinmail.com. Bath, hot water, basic, clean, friendly, rooms on top floor are baked by the sun, one of the cheapest, popular with locals, will store luggage, good cheap meals available, local speciality *poc chuc*.

Camping

Trailer Park Rainbow, Km 8, on the road to Progreso, T999-926 1026. US$18 for 1 or 2, hot showers, all facilities and good bus connection into town. Reports of excessive charging for use of amenities.

Celestún *p37*

Most lodgings are along Calle 12.

$$$$ Hotel Eco Paraíso Xixim, Km 10 off the old Sisal Hwy, T988-916 2100, www.ecoparaiso.com. In coconut grove on edge of reserve, pool, tours to surrounding area including flamingos, turtle nesting, etc.

$$ Gutiérrez, Calle 12 (the Malecón) No 127, T988-916 2609. Large beds, fans, views, clean.

$ San Julio, Calle 12 No 92, T988-916 2062. Large bright rooms and clean bathrooms, owner knowledgeable about the area.

Progreso and around *p38*
$$-$ Tropical Suites, Calle 19 No 143, T969-935 1263. Suites and rooms with cable TV, a/c, sea views.
$ Progreso, Calle 29 No 142, T969-935 0039. Simple rooms in the centre.

Ticul and Oxkutzcab *p40*
$$ Trujeque, Calle 48 No 102-A, Oxkutzcab, T997-975 0568. A/c, TV, clean, good value, discount for stays over a week.
$ Casa de Huéspedes, near bus terminal, Oxkutzcab. Large rooms with bath, TV, fan, friendly. Recommended.
$ Hotel Rosalía, Calle 54 No 101 Oxkutzcab, T997-975 0167, turn right out of bus station, right again. Double room, shower, cable TV.
$ Motel Bugambilias, Calle 23 No 291, Ticul, T997-972 1368. Clean, basic rooms.
$ Sierra Sosa, Calle 26, near zócalo, Ticul, T997-972 0008. Cheap rooms that are dungeon-like, but friendly, clean and helpful.

Uxmal *p42*
There is no village at Uxmal, just the following hotels. For cheap accommodation, go to Ticul, 28 km away (see above).
$$$$ The Lodge at Uxmal, entrance to ruins, T997-976 2102, www.mayaland.com/Lodge Uxmal. Same owners as **Hacienda Uxmal**. Comfortable, a/c, bath, TV, fair restaurant.
$$$ Hacienda Uxmal, T997-976 2012, www.mayaland.com/HaciendaUxmal, 300-400 m from ruins. Good, efficient and relaxing, good Yucatecan restaurant, a/c, gardens, pool.
$$$ Misión Uxmal, 1-2 km from ruins on Mérida road, Km 78, T997-976 2022, www.hotelesmision.com.mx. Rooms are a bit dark, with a pool.
$$$ Villas Arqueológicas de Uxmal, Carretera Mérida–Uxmal, Km 78, about

12 km north of ruins, T997-976 2040, www.villasarqueo logicas.com.mx. Boutique-style new hotel, with bird-watching and jungle tour packages.
$$ Rancho Uxmal, Carretera Mérida–Uxmal, Km 70, about 4 km north of ruins, T997-977 6254. Comfortable rooms, hot and cold water, camping for US$5, pool, reasonable food but not cheap (no taxis to get there).
$$-$ Sacbé Hostel, at Km 127 on Hwy 261, T997-858 1281. A mix of private rooms (private bath), dorms and campsite, with space for hammocks, and solar-powered showers, with breakfast and dinner for a little more.

Camping
No camping allowed at the site, but there is a campsite at **Sacbé Hostel**, see above. 2nd-class buses from Mérida to Campeche pass by, ask to be let out at the **Campo de Baseball**. French and Mexican owners, beautiful park, fastidiously clean and impeccably managed. 9 electric hook-ups (US$7-10 for motor home according to size), big area for tents (US$2.75 per person with tent), *palapas* for hammocks (US$2.65 per person), for cars pay US$1, showers, toilets, clothes-washing facilities, also 3 bungalows with ceiling fan (**$**), breakfast, vegetarian lunch and dinner available (US$2.65 each). Highly recommended.

Izamal and around *p42*
$$ Macan-Che, Calle 22 No 305 between Calle 33 and 35, T988-954 0287, www.macanche.com. 4 blocks north of plaza, pleasant bungalows, breakfast. Recommended.

Chichén Itzá *p43*
$$$$ Hacienda Chichén, T999-924 8407, www.haciendachichen.com. Luxury resort and spa, close to the ruins, with tasteful rooms, suites and bungalows. There's a garden, library and restaurant, all contained by historic colonial grounds.

$$$ Villas Arqueológicas, T997-974 6020, Apdo Postal 495, Mérida, www.villasarqueologicas.com.mx. Close to the ruins. Pool, tennis, restaurant (expensive and poor). Both are on the other side of the fenced-off ruins from the bus stop; either walk all the way round, or take taxi (US$1-1.50).

$$$-$$ Hotel Chichén Itzá, Piste, T999-851 0022, www.mayaland.com. 3 types of rooms and tariffs. The best are clean, tasteful, overlook the garden and have a/c, internet, phone and fridge. Cheaper rooms overlook the street.

$$ Dolores Alba Chichén, Km 122, T985-858 1555, www.doloresalba.com. Small, Spanish-owned hotel, 2.5 km on the road to Puerto Juárez (bus passes it), 40 clean bungalows with shower, a/c and cable TV. Pool, restaurant, English is spoken. Sister hotel in Mérida.

$$ Pirámide Inn Resort, 1.5 km from ruins, at the Chichén end of Piste, Km 117, T999-851 0115, www.chichen.com. This long-standing Piste favourite has been remodelled. It has many clean, comfortable rooms, a pool, hammocks and *palapas*. Temazcal available, book 24 hrs in advance. Camping costs US$5, or US$15 with a car. Friendly owner, speaks English.

$$ Posada Maya, Calle 8 No 70, just off the main road. Small, simple rooms, desperately in need of a deep clean. However, there's space to sling a hammock if you're terribly impoverished (**$**).

$$ Posada Olalde, 100 m from the main road at the end of Calle 6, between Calle 15 and 17. This lovely, family-run hotel has a handful of economical rooms and basic Yucatecan *cabañas* built the old-fashioned way. There's a lush, tranquil garden and the Mayan owners are kind and friendly.

$ Stardust Posada Annex, Piste, about 2 km before the ruins if coming from Mérida (taxi to ruins US$2.50). Simple, basic rooms and a range of tariffs to suit your budget. Slightly run-down, but acceptable. There's also a pool and an average restaurant.

Valladolid *p45, map p46*

$$$ Mesón del Marqués, Calle 39 with Calle 40 and 42, north side of Plaza Principal, T985-856 2073, www.mesondelmarques.com. Housed in a handsome colonial edifice, this hotel has 90 tasteful rooms, all with a/c and cable TV. There's a swimming pool, Wi-Fi, garden and laundry service. Recommended.

$$$-$$ María de la Luz, Calle 42 No 193-C, Plaza Principal, T985-856 1181, www.mariadelaluz hotel.com. Good clean rooms, tours to Chichén Itzá and Río Lagartos, excellent restaurant.

$$ María Guadalupe, Calle 44 No 198, T985-856 2068. Simple, clean rooms with fan. Good value, hot water, washing facilities. Recommended.

$$ San Clemente, Calle 42 No 206, T985-856 2208, www.hotelsanclemente.com.mx. Many clean, comfortable rooms with a/c (cheaper with fan) and cable TV. There's a pool, restaurant, garden and free parking. Recommended.

$ Albergue La Candelaria, Calle 35 No 201-F, T985-856 2267, candelaria_hostel@ hotmail.com. Good cheap option, especially for solo travellers. Single-sex dorms with fan, clean, hot water, kitchen, washing facilities, hammocks out the back in the garden, TV room. Recommended.

$ Antonio 'Negro' Aguilar rents rooms for 2, 3 or 4 people. The best budget deal in the town for 2 or more, clean, spacious rooms on a quiet street, garden, volleyball/ basketball court. The rooms are on Calle 41 No 225, before the **Maya Hotel**, but you need to book them at Aguilar's shop (Calle 44 No 195, T985-856 2125). If the shop's closed, knock on the door of the house on the right of the shop.

$ Hostal del Fraile, Calle de los Frailes 212-C, T985-856 5852. Youth hostal with 20 beds, free breakfast, clean, quiet, friendly. Best budget lodgings in town.

Río Lagartos and around *p47*

$$ Villa de Pescadores, Calles 14 No 93, on the Malecón T986-862 0020. 9 rooms, best hotel in town, friendly and helpful.

$ Tere and Miguel, near the harbour (ask at the bus terminal). 3 rooms for rent, very nicely furnished, double and triple rooms, 1 with an extra hammock, sea views.

Eating

Mérida *p34, map p36*

There are a number of taco stands, pizzerias and sandwich places in Pasaje Picheta, a small plaza off the Palacio de Gobierno.

$$$ Alberto's Continental, Calle 64 No 482 corner Calle 57. Yucatecan, Lebanese and international food, mouth-watering steaks and seafood, all inside a colonial mansion. Highly recommended.

$$$ Casa de Piedra 'Xcanatún', in Hacienda Xcanatún (see Sleeping), Km 12 Carretera Mérida–Progreso, T999-941 0213. Fine dining, best restaurant in the area (although a bit out of town). Popular with locals. Reserve if possible. Highly recommended.

$$$ Villa María, Calle 59 No 553 and Calle 68, T999-923 3357, www.villamariamerida.com. Classical music spills over the white tablecloths at this sophisticated, fine-dining establishment. The interior is beautiful and they serve French, Mediterranean and Mexican cuisine.

$$$-$ Café La Habana, Calle 59 y Calle 62. Neither the coffee nor the food is fantastic, but it's OK for a snack. A fine spot for people-watching, open 24 hrs. Free Wi-Fi.

$$ El Nuevo Tucho, Calle 60 near University. Good local dishes, mostly meat and fish, and occasional live music. Healthy and extensive drinks menu. Evening entertainment also.

$$ La Casa de Frida, Calle 61, between Calle 66 and 66A, www.lacasadefrida.com.mx. Mon-Sat 1800-2200. Frida Kahlo-themed restaurant in a colourful courtyard setting, traditional Mexican cuisine, including *mole* and *chiles en nogada*.

$$ Los Almendros, Calle 50A No 493 esq 59. Housed in a high-vaulted, white-washed thatched barn, this award-winning restaurant specializes in 1st-rate traditional Yucatecan cuisine, serving tasty dishes like *pollo pibil* and *poc chuc*. Confusingly, the entrance is through the car park.

$$ Pórtico del Peregrino, Calle 57 between Calle 60 and 62. Dining indoors or in an attractive leafy courtyard, excellent food.

$$-$ Amaro, Calle 59 No 507 between Calle 60 and 62, near the plaza. Open late daily. With open courtyard and covered patio, good food, especially vegetarian, try *chaya* drink from the leaf of the *chaya* tree; their curry, avocado pizza and home-made bread are also very good.

$$-$ Café Chocolate, Calle 60 No 442 y Calle 49, T999-928 5113, www.cafe-chocolate. com.mx. This café and art space does good *mole*, as well as an excellent breakfast buffet, a lunchtime menu and evening meals. They also have home-made fresh bread and pasta, and an excellent selection of fruit drinks and teas. Cosy and classy at the same time, with antique furniture, free Wi-Fi and art and photography exhibitions in beautiful surroundings, with sofas indoors or outdoor courtyard seating. Highly recommended.

$$-$ Flor de Santiago, Calle 70 No 478, between Calle 57 and 59. Reputedly the oldest restaurant in Mérida. There's a cafeteria and bakery in one section, serving cheap snacks and à la carte meals. The patio out back is sophisticated and serves Yucatecan specialities. Breakfast buffet is good value.

$$-$ La Vía Olympo (formerly **La Valentina**) on main plaza opposite cathedral. Good-value Mexican and Yucatecan dishes, brisk service and outdoor seating. Good for breakfasts, free Wi-Fi.

$$-$ Restaurant Colonial, Calle 62 and 57. Average coffee, but this place lays on an 'all you can eat' breakfast buffet for US$6, with fruit, coffee, good juice, eggs, cereal and other offerings. Fill up on several courses and then come back for the lunch buffet – this time there are steaks, but drinks aren't included.

$ Café Alameda, Calle 58 No 474 between Calle 57 and 55. Arabic and Mexican cuisine, breakfast and lunch only, 0730-1700.

$ El Trapiche, near on Calle 62 half a block north of the plaza. Good local dishes, excellent pizzas, sandwiches, omelettes, *tortas*, tacos, burgers and freshly made juices.

$ Marlín Azul, Calle 62, between Calle 57 and 59. The place for cheap seafood fare, mostly frequented by locals. Get a shrimp cocktail breakfast for a couple of dollars.

$ Marys, Calle 63 No 486, between Calle 63 and 58. Mainly Mexican customers. Possibly the cheapest joint in town. *Comida corrida* for US$2.50. Recommended.

$ Mérida, Calle 62 between Calle 59 and 61. Full 3 course for US$2.50 – a bargain, and it's tasty Yucatecan fare as well.

$ Vito Corleone's Pizza, Calle 59 No 508, between Calle 62 and 60. Open from 1800. Serves pop and pizza, by the slice or whole, eat in or take away. Popular with students and young Mexicans.

Cafés, juices and ice cream parlours

Café El Hoyo, Calle 62, between Calle 57 and 59. A chilled out spot with a patio, popular with students, serving coffee, beer and snacks.

Café Petropolis, Calle 70 opposite CAME terminal. Existed long before the terminal was built, family-run, turkey a speciality, excellent quality, good *horchata* and herb teas.

El Colón Sorbetes y Dulces Finos, Calle 61 and 60. Serving ice cream since 1907, great sorbets, *meringue*, good menu with explanation of fruits in English. Highly recommended. About 30 different flavours of good ice cream.

Italian Coffee Company, Calle 62 between Calle 59 and 61. A bit like a Mexican Starbucks, but nevertheless serves excellent coffee, decent toasted baguettes, and tasty cakes for those feeling a trifle decadent.

Jugos California, Calle 62 and 63 good fruit salads and juices. Next door **Jugos Janitzio** also good.

There's a good *panadería* at Calle 62 y 61. Parque Santa Ana, is good for cheap street fare. Closed middle of the day.

Celestún *p37*

Many beachside restaurants along Calle 12, but be careful of food in the cheaper ones; recommended is **La Playita**, for fried fish, seafood cocktails. Food stalls along Calle 11 beside the bus station should be approached with caution.

$$ Chivirico, across the road from **La Playita**, offers descent fish, shrimp and other seafood.

$$ El Lobo, Calle 10 and 13, on the corner of the main square. Best spot for breakfast, with fruit salads, yoghurt, pancakes, etc. Celestún's best pizza in the evenings.

Progreso and around *p38*

The Malecón at Progreso is lined with seafood restaurants, some with tables on the beach. For cheaper restaurants, head for the centre of town, near the bus terminal.

$$-$ Las Palmas and **El Cocalito** are 2 of several reasonable fish restaurants in Chelem.

$ Casablanca, **Capitan Marisco** and **Le Saint Bonnet**, Malecón, Progreso, all recommended.

Ticul and Oxkutzcab *p40*

♉ Los Almendros, Calle 23 207, Ticul. Nice colonial building with patio, good Yucatecan cuisine, reasonable prices.

♉ Pizzería La Góndola, Calle 23, Ticul. Good, moderately priced pizzas.

$ El Colorín, near **Hotel Sierra Sosa** on Calle 26, Ticul. Cheap local food.

Uxmal *p42*

$$$-$$ Restaurant at ruins, good but expensive.

Izamal and around *p42*

There are several restaurants on Plaza
de la Constitución.

$$ Kinich-Kakmó, Calle 27 No 299 between
Calle 28 and 30. Near ruins of same name,
local food.

$$ Tumben-Lol, Calle 22 No 302 between
Calle 31 and 33. Yucatecan cuisine.

$ El Norteño at bus station. Good and cheap.

$ Wayane, near statue of Diego de Landa.
Friendly, clean.

Chichén Itzá *p43*

Mostly poor and overpriced in Chichén itself
(cafés inside the ruins are cheaper than the
restaurant at the entrance, but still expensive).
Restaurants in Pisté close 2100-2200.

$$ Fiesta Maya, Calle 15 No 59, Pisté.
Reportedly the best restaurant in town. Serves
Yucatecan food, tacos, meat and sandwiches.
Lunch buffet every day at 1200, US$10.

$ Pollo Mexicano on the main road in Pisté.
One of several simple places that serves
mouth-watering, barbequed chicken.

$ Sayil in Pisté. Serves Yucatecan dishes like
pollo pibil, as well as breakfast *huevos al gusto*.

Valladolid *p45, map p46*

There is a well-stocked supermarket on the
road between the centre and bus station.

$$ El Mesón del Marqués, Calle 39, between
Calle 40 and 42. Award-winning restaurant
serving seafood and Yucatecan cuisine in a
tranquil setting. Intimate and romantic.

$$ La Sirenita, Calle 34N, between Calle 29
and 31, T985-856 1655, few blocks east of
main square. Closes 1800, closed Sun.
Highly recommended for seafood, popular
and friendly.

$$ Plaza Maya, Calle 41 No 235, a few blocks
east of main square. Great regional food and
good *comida corrida*, step up from the rest.

$ Bazar, northeast corner of Plaza
Principal, next to Mesón del Marqués.
Wholesome grub.

Cafés

Las Campanas, Calle 41 and 42, opposite
the plaza, serves various types of coffee.

Río Lagartos and around *p47*

For a fishing village, the seafood is not
spectacular, as most of the good fish is
sold to restaurants in Mérida and Cancún.

$$ Isla Contoy, Calle 19 No 134. Average
seafood, not cheap for the quality.

$$ Los Negritos, off the plaza. Moderately
priced seafood.

🎭 Entertainment

Mérida *p34, map p36*

See the free listings magazine *Yucatán Today*.

Bars and clubs

There are several good bars on the north
side of the plaza, beer is moderately priced
at US$1, although food can be expensive.
There are a number of live-music venues
around Parque Santa Lucía, a couple of
blocks from the main plaza.

El Cielo, Paseo de Montejo and Calle 25,
T999-944 5127, www.elcielobar.com. Sexy,
white leather lounge-bar that plays house,
techno and pop. Don your dancing shoes and
say 'buenas noches' to the beautiful people.

El Tucho, also known as **El Nuevo Tucho**,
Calle 55 between 60 and 58. A restaurant
open till 2100 only, with live music, often
guest performers from Cuba play. Good
food as well.

La Parranda, Calle 60, between 59 and 61,
T999-938 0435, laparrandamerida.com.
This touristy cantina is always buzzing with
atmosphere in the evenings. Live music
Thu-Sat and always a steady flow of beer.

Mambo Café, Plaza Las Americanas
Shopping Mall, T999-987 7533, www.mambo
cafe.com.mx. Big club in Mérida, mainly salsa
but all kinds of music. Wed-Sat from 2100.

Panchos, Calle 59 between Calle 60 and 62.
Very touristy, staff in traditional gear,
but lively and busy, live music, patio.

Cinema

There is a cinema showing subtitled films in English on Parque Hidalgo.
Teatro Mérida, Calle 62 between 59 and 61, shows European, Mexican and independent movies as well as live theatre productions. The 14-screen multiplex **Cinepolis** is in the huge Plaza de las Américas, north of the city; *colectivo* and buses take 20 mins and leave from Calle 65 between 58 and 60. **Hollywood Cinema**, near Parque Santiago, has 4 screens.

Theatre

Teatro Peón Contreras, Calle 60 with 57. Shows start at 2100, US$4, ballet, etc.

✹ Festivals and events

Mérida *p34, map p36*
Every **Thu** there is a cultural music and dance show in Plaza Santa Lucía. **Sat** brings **En El Corazón de Mérida**, with music and dance in bars, restaurants and in the street. Every **Sun** the central streets are closed off to traffic, live music and parades abound.
6 Jan Mérida celebrates its birthday.
Feb/Mar Carnival takes place the week before Ash Wed (best on Sat). Floats, dancers in regional costume, music and dancing around the plaza and children dressed in animal suits.

Chichén Itzá *p43*

21 Mar and 21 Sep On the morning and afternoon of the spring and autumn equinoxes, the alignment of the sun's shadow casts a serpentine image on the side of the steps of El Castillo. This occasion is popular and you'll be lucky to get close enough to see the action. Note that this phenomenon can also be seen on the days before and after the equinox, 19th-23rd of the month.

Río Lagartos *p47*

17 Jul A big local **fiesta**, with music, food and dancing in the plaza.

12 Dec Virgen de Guadalupe.
The whole village converges on the chapel built in 1976 on the site of a vision of the Virgin Mary by a local non-believer, who suddenly died, along with his dog, shortly after receiving the vision.

⊙ Shopping

Mérida *p34, map p36*
Bookshops
Amate, Calle 60 453A, between 49 and 51, T999-924 2222, www.amatebooks.com. You'll find a superb stock of literature here, covering everything from architecture to Yucatecan cuisine, but anthropology, archaeology, history and art are the mainstay. Another branch in Oaxaca.
Librerías Dante, Calle 59, No 498 between 58 and 60. Also Calle 61 between 62 and 64 (near **Lavandería La Fe**), used books.

Crafts and souvenirs
You'll find an abundance of craft shops in the streets around the plaza. They sell hammocks (see box, page 38), silver jewellery, Panama hats, *guayabera* shirts, *huaraches*, baskets and Maya figurines. The salesmen are ruthless, but they expect to receive about half their original asking price. Bargain hard, but maintain good humour, patience and face. And watch out for the many touts around the plaza, using all sorts of ingenious ploys to get you to their shops.

There are 2 main craft markets in the city: the **Mercado Municipal**, Calle 56a and 67 and the **García Rejón Bazaar**, also known as **Casa de la Artesanía**, Calle 65 and 60. The former sprawls, smells and takes over several blocks, but it's undeniably alive and undeniably Mexican. It sells everything under the sun and is also good for a cheap, tasty meal, but check the stalls for cleanliness. The latter is excellent for handicrafts and renowned for clothing, particularly leather *huaraches* and good-value cowboy boots – good, cheap Yucatecan fare.

If you're looking for a hammock, several places are recommended, but shop around for the best deal. **El Mayab**, Calle 58 No 553 and 71, are friendly, have a limited choice but good deals available; **La Poblana**, Calle 65 between Calle 58 and 60, will bargain, especially for sales of more than 1 – they have a huge stock. **El Aguacate**, Calle 58 No 604, corner of Calle 73, good hammocks and no hard sell. Recommended. **Casa de Artesanías Ki-Huic**, Calle 63, between Calle 62 and 64, is a friendly store with all sorts of handicrafts from silver and wooden masks, to hammocks and batik. Shop owner Julio Chay is very knowledgeable and friendly, sometimes organizes trips for visitors to his village, Tixkokob, which specializes in hammocks. Open daily, 0900-2100. Julio can also organize trips to other nearby villages and the shop has tequilas for sampling.

For silver, there are a handful of stores on Calle 60, just north of the plaza.

Mexican folk art, including *calaveras* (Day of the Dead skeletons), is available from **Minaturas**, Calle 59 No 507A; and **Yalat**, Calle 39 and 40.

If you're in the market for a *guayabera* shirt, you'll find stores all over the city, particularly on Calle 62, between 57 and 61.

Supermarkets
Supermaz, Calle 56, between 65 and 63.

Progreso and around *p38*
Mundo Marino, Calle 80 s/n, 1 block from the beach, T969-915 1380. Shark-related souvenirs.

Izamal and around *p42*
Hecho a mano, Calle 31 No 332 between 36 and 38. Folk art, postcards, textiles, jewellery, papier-mâché masks.
Market, Calle 31, on Plaza de la Constitución, opposite convent, closes soon after lunch.

▲ Activities and tours

Mérida *p34, map p36*
Tour operators
Most tour operators can arrange trips to popular local destinations including Chichén Itzá, Uxmal, Celestún and nearby *cenotes*.
Amigo Yucatán, Av Colón No 508-C and offices in 3 hotels, T999-920 0104, www.amigoyucatan.com. Interesting gastronomy and tasting tours of Yucatán, as well as excursions to Maya ruins, Izamal, Puuc Route and Celestún. It's possible to book all tours online, 24 hrs in advance recommended, but also possible before 0830 on the same day (best to do this in person or on the phone). Friendly. Recommended.
Carmen Travel Services, Calle 27 No 151, between 32 and 34, T999-927 2027, www.carmentravel.com, 3 other branches. This well-established agency can organize flights, hotels and all the usual trips to the sights. Recommended.
Ecoturismo Yucatán, Calle 3 No 235, between Calle 32A and 34, T999-920 2772, www.ecoyuc.com.mx. Specializes in educational and ecotourism tours including jungle trips, birding expeditions and turtle-hatching tours. Also offers adventure and archaeological packages.
Yucatan Connection, Calle 33 No 506, T999-163 8224, www.yucatan-connection.com. Tours to lesser visited Mayan sites like Mayapán, Tecoh and Ochil. Staff are fluent in English, Czech and Slovak.
Yucatán Trails, Calle 62, No 482, Av 57-59, T999-928 2582, www.yucatantrails.com. Canadian owner Denis Lafoy is friendly, English-speaking and helpful. He runs tours to all the popular local destinations, stores luggage cheaply, has a book exchange and throws famous parties on the 1st Fri of every month.

Mérida *p34, map p36*
Air
Aeropuerto Rejón (MID), 8 km from town. From Calle 67, 69 and 60, bus 79 goes to the airport, marked 'Aviación', US$0.35, roughly every 20 mins. Taxi set price voucher system US$8; *colectivo* US$2.50. Good domestic flight connections. International flight connections with **Belize City**, **Houston**, **Miami** and **Havana**. Package tours Mérida–Havana–Mérida available (be sure to have a confirmed return flight). For return to Mexico ask for details at Secretaría de Migración Av Colón and Calle 8.

Airline offices Aerolínenas Aztecas, T01-800-229-8322. **AeroMéxico**, Av Colón 451 and Montejo, T999-920 1260, www.aeromexico.com. **Aviacsa**, T999-925 6890, www.aviasca.com.mx. **Aviateca**, T999-926 9087. **Continental**, T999-926 3100, www.continental.com. **Delta**, T01-800-123-410, www.delta.com.

Bus
There are several bus terminals in Mérida.

The **CAME terminal** Buses to destinations outside Yucatán State, Chichén Itzá and Valladolid operating **ADO** and **UNO** buses leave from the 1st-class CAME terminal at Calle 70, No 555, between Calle 69 and 71. The station has lockers and is open 24 hrs, left luggage charges from US$0.30 per bag, depending on size. About 20 mins' walk to centre, taxi US$2.50. Schedules change frequently.

The **ADO terminal** Around the corner, has left luggage open 24 hrs, and is for Yucatán destinations except Chichén Itzá with fleets run by **Mayab**, **ATS**, **Sur** and **Oriente**.

There are also 1st-class departures from the **Hotel Fiesta Americana**, Calle 60 and Colón, which are mostly luxury services to Cancún.

Buses to **Progreso** depart every 15 mins, US$1.50, from their own terminal at Calle 62 No 524, between 65 and 67.

There is another 2nd-class terminal near the market at Calle 50 and 65. It deals with obscure local destinations, including **Timzimín**, **Cenotillo**, **Izamal** and many Maya villages specializing in different crafts, including **Tixkokob**.

To **Cancún**, hourly 1st-class ADO services, 4 hrs, US$18, and frequent 2nd-class services, US$15. To **Campeche**, frequent **ADO** and 2nd-class services, 2 hrs, US$7-10. To **Chichén Itzá** (ruins and Pisté), **ADO** services at 0630, 0915, 1240, 2 hrs, US$7, and cheaper, frequent 2nd-class buses stop on their way to Cancún. To **Celestún**, frequent 2nd-class **Oriente** services, 2 hrs, US$3.50. To **Coatzacoalcos**, ADO services at 1210, 1830, 1930 and 2130, 12 hrs, US$38. To **Palenque**, ADO services at 0830, 1915, 2200, 8 hrs, US$26. To **Ruta Puuc**, 2nd-class ATS service, 0800, US$10. To **Tulum**, ADO services at 0630, 1040, 1240, 1745, 1945, 6 hrs, US$9-14. To **Uxmal**, 2nd-class SUR services at 0600, 0905, 1040, 1205, 1705, 1½ hrs, US$3. To **Valladolid**, hourly ADO services, 1½ hrs, US$9, and 5 2nd-class buses, all in the afternoon and evening, US$5.50. To **Villahermosa**, frequent ADO services, 9 hrs, US$30.50 and several ADO GL services, US$36. To **Tuxtla Guitérrez**, an OCC service at 1915, 15 hrs, US$40, and ADO GL services at 1900 and 2315, US$55. To **San Cristóbal de las Casas**, an OCC service at 1915, 13 hrs, US$36. To **Tenosique**, an ADO service at 2100, US$29.

To Guatemala Take a bus from Mérida to San Cristóbal and change there for Comitán, or to Tenosique for the route to Flores. Another alternative would be to take the bus from Mérida direct to Tuxtla Gutiérrez (times given above), then connect to Cd Cuauhtémoc or to Tapachula.

To Belize Take a bus to **Chetumal**, ADO services at 0730 (except Wed and Sat),

1300, 1800, 2300, 6 hrs, US$21 and cross the border. **Premier** operate services from Chetumal to **Belize City** at 1145, 1445 and 1745, 5 hrs, US$10, schedules are subject to change.

Car

Car hire Car reservations should be booked well in advance if possible. Hire firms charge around US$45-50 a day although bargains can be found in low season. All agencies allow vehicles to be returned to Cancún for an extra charge, and most have an office at the airport where they share the same counter and negotiating usually takes place. Agencies include: **Budget**, at the airport, T999-946 1323; **Executive**, Calle 56A No 451, corner of Av Colón, at the Hotel Fiesta Americana, T999-925 8171, www.executive. com.mx; **Easy Way Car Rental**, Calle 60, between 55 and 57, T999-930 9500, www.easywayrentacar-yucatan.com; **Mexico Rent a Car**, Calle 57 A Depto 12, between 58 and 60, T999-923 3637, mexicorentacar@hotmail.com.

Car service Servicios de Mérida Goodyear, Calle 59, near Av 68. Very helpful, competent, owner speaks English, good coffee while you wait for your vehicle. Honest car servicing or quick oil change.

Taxi

There are 2 types: the Volkswagens, which you can flag down, prices range from US$3.50-7; cheaper are the 24-hr radio taxis, T999-928 5328, or catch 1 from their kiosk on Parque Hidalgo. In both types of taxi, establish fare before journey; there are set prices depending on the distance, the minimum is an expensive US$2.50 even for a few blocks.

Celestún p37

Bus Buses leave every 1-2 hrs from the local bus station on Calle 65 between 50 and 52, in Mérida, 2-hr journey, 1st class US$3.50, 2nd class US$3.

Progreso and around p38

Boat Boats can be hired to visit the reef of **Los Alacranes** where many ancient wrecks are visible in clear water.

Bus Buses from **Mérida** leave from the terminal on Calle 62 between 67 and 65, next to Hotel La Paz, every 10 mins. US$0.80 1-way/ US$2 return. Returns every 10 mins until 2200.

Dzibilchaltún p39

Bus 5 direct buses a day on weekdays, from Parque San Juan, marked 'Tour/Ruta Polígono'; returns from the site entrance on the hour, passing the junction 15 mins later, taking 45 mins from the junction to **Mérida** (US$0.60).

Shuttles Leave from Parque San Juan in Mérida, corner of Calle 62 y 67A, every 1 or 2 hrs between 0500 and 1900.

Ticul and Oxkutzcab p40

Colectivo There are frequent VW colectivos to Ticul from Parque San Juan, **Mérida**, US$2.50.

Uxmal p42

Bus 5 buses a day from **Mérida**, from the terminal on Calle 69 between Calle 68 and 70, US$4. Return buses run every 2 hrs, or go to the entrance to the site on the main road and wait for a colectivo, which will take you to Muná for US$0.50. From there, many buses (US$1.70) and colectivos (US$1.40) go to Mérida.

Car Parking at the site costs US$1 for the whole day. Uxmal is 74 km from **Mérida**, 177 km from **Campeche**, by a good paved road. If going by car from Mérida, there is a circular road round the city: follow the signs to Campeche, then 'Campeche via ruinas', then to 'Muná via Yaxcopoil' (long stretch of road with no signposting). Muná–Yaxcopoil is about 34 km. Parking US$1.

Izamal and around *p42*

Bus Bus station is on Calle 32 behind government offices, can leave bags. 2nd class to **Mérida**, every 45 mins, 1½ hrs, US$1.50, lovely countryside. Bus station in Mérida, Calle 67 between 50 and 52. 6 a day to/from **Valladolid** (96 km), about 2 hrs, US$2.30-3.

Chichén Itzá *p43*

ADO bus office in Pisté is between **Stardust** and **Pirámide Inn**. Budget travellers going on from Mérida to Isla Mujeres or Cozumel should visit Chichén from Valladolid (see below), although if you plan to go through in a day you can store luggage at the visitor centre.

Bus Frequent 2nd-class buses depart from Mérida to Cancún, passing Chichén Itzá and Pisté. Likewise, there are frequent departures to/from Valladolid. The bus station in Pisté is between Stardust and Pirámide Inn. To **Mérida**, 2nd class, hourly, US$5; and 1st class, 1420 and 1720, US$7. To **Cancún**, 2nd class, hourly, US$9. To **Valladolid**, 2nd class, hourly, US$2.50. To **Tulum**, 2nd class, 0810, 1420, 1615, US$11. The ruins are a 5-min ride from Pisté – the buses drop off and pick up passengers until 1700 at the top of the coach station opposite the entrance.

Valladolid *p45, map p46*

Bus The main bus terminal is on Calle 37 and Calle 54. To **Cancún**, ADO, frequent, 2½ hrs, US$9; and many 2nd class, 3-4 hrs, US$5.50. To **Chichén Itzá**, ADO, many daily, 30 mins; US$3; and many 2nd class, US$1.50. To **Mérida**, ADO, 16 daily, 2½ hrs, US$9. To **Playa del Carmen**, 1st and 2nd class, 11 daily, 3½ hrs, US$8.50. To **Tizimín** (for Río Lagartos), frequent 1 hr, US$1.30. To **Tulum**, frequent ADO and ATS services, 3 hrs, US$5.

Río Lagartos and around *p47*

Bus There are 2 terminals side by side in Tizimín. If coming from Valladolid en route to Río Lagartos, you will need to walk to the other terminal. Tizimín–Río Lagartos, 7 per day, 1½ hrs, US$2. To **Valladolid**, frequent, 1 hr, US$1.30. To **Mérida**, several daily, 4 hrs, US$4. There are also buses to **Cancún**, **Felipe Carrillo Puerto** and **Chetumal**.

It is possible to get to Río Lagartos and back in a day from **Valladolid**, if you leave on the 0630 or 0730 bus (taxi Tizimín–Río Lagartos US$25, driver may negotiate). Last bus back from Río Lagartos at 1730.

⊙ Directory

Mérida *p34, map p36*

Banks Banamex, at Calle 56 and 59 (Mon-Fri 0900-1300, 1600-1700), ATM cash machine. Many banks on Calle 65, off the plaza. Most have ATM cash machines, open 24 hrs. The beautiful **Casa de Montejo**, on the main plaza is also a Banamex branch. Open 0900-1600, Mon-Fri. **HSBC** usually changes TCs and stays open later than other banks, 0900-1900, Mon-Fri and 0900-1500 Sat. **Cultural centres** Alliance Française, Calle 56 No 476 between 55 and 57, T999-927 2403. Has a busy programme of events, films (Thu 1900), a library and a *cafetería* open all day. **Embassies and consulates** Austria, Av Colón No 59, T999-925 6386. Belize, Calle 53 No 498, corner of 58, T999-928 6152. **Cuba**, Calle 42 No 200, T999-944 4216. **France**, Calle 60 No 385, between 41 and 43, T999-930 1542. Germany, Calle 49 No 212, between 30 and 32, T999-944 3252. **Honduras**, Instituto Monte Líbano, Calle 54 No 486, between 57 and 59, T999-926 1922. **Netherlands**, Calle 64 No 418 between 47 and 49, T999-924 3122. **USA**, Calle 60 No 338, T999-942 5700. **Internet** Multitude of internet cafés, most charging US$1-1.50. **Language schools** Centro de Idiomas del Sureste, Calle 52 No 455, between 49 and 51, T999-923 0083, www.cisyucatan.com.mx, is a well-established Spanish school offering tried and tested language and cultural programmes. **Modern Spanish Institute**,

Calle 15 No 500B, between 16A and 18, T999-911 0790, www.modernspanish.com, courses in Spanish, Maya culture, homestays. **Laundry** Lavandería, Calle 69 No 541, 2 blocks from bus station, about US$4.50 a load, 3-hr service. **La Fe**, Calle 61, No 518, between 62 and 64. US$4.50 for 3 kg. Highly recommended (shoe repair next door). Self-service hard to find. **Libraries** Mérida English Library, Calle 53 No 524 between 66 and 68, T999-924 8401, www.meridaenglish library.com. Many books on Mexico, used book for sale, bulletin board, magazines, reading patio. Mon-Fri 0900-1300; Mon 1830-2100; Thu 1600-1900; Sat 1000-1300. **Medical services** Hospitals: Centro Médico de las Américas (CEMA), Calle 54 No 365 between 33A and Av Pérez Ponce, T999-926 2111, emergencies T999-927 3199, www.cmasureste.com, affiliated with **Mercy Hospital**, Miami, Florida, US. **Red Cross**, T999-924 9813. **Dentists: Dr Javier Cámara Patrón**, Calle 17 No 170, between 8 and 10, T999-925 3399, www.dentistyucatan.com. **Post** Calle 53, between 52 and 54. Will accept parcels for surface mail to US only, but don't seal parcels destined overseas; they have to be inspected. For surface mail to Europe try Belize, or mail package to US, Poste Restante, for collection later if you are heading that way. **Telephone** International calls are possible from caseta telefónicas. You'll find them all over town, but especially on Calle 62 and 60, north of the plaza. Calls to Europe cost around 4 pesos per min, 2-3 pesos to the USA.

___

Izamal and around *p42*
Banks Bank on square with statue to Fray Diego de Landa, south side of convent. **Post** On opposite side of square to convent.

___

Chichén Itzá *p43*
Banks ATMs on the main street. **Internet** Available in Pisté. **Telephone** International calls may be placed from **Teléfonos de México**, opposite Hotel Xaybe.

___

Valladolid *p45, map p46*
Banks Santander Serfin, Calle 39 No 229; Bancomer, Calle 40 No 196; HSBC, Calle 41 No 201; Banamex, Calle 42, No 206. **Internet** Phonet, west side of the plaza, daily 1000-2100, internet costs US$1 per hr and there are long-distance call facilities. There are many other internet cafés. **Laundry** Teresita, Calle 33 between 40 and 42, US$6 for 5.5 kg. **Post** On east side of plaza, 0800-1500 (does not accept parcels for abroad). **Telephone** Telmex phone office on Calle 42, just north of square; expensive **Computel** offices at bus station and next to Hotel San Clemente; **Ladatel** phonecards can be bought from *farmacias* for use in phone booths.

State of Quintana Roo

The burgeoning international destinations of Cancún, Playa del Carmen, Isla Mujeres and Cozumel overshadow the eastern coast of the Yucatán and the State of Quintana Roo. Resorts: you either love them, hate them or simply enjoy the beautiful beaches, package tours and reliable restaurants. If Cancún is your port of entry for a trip through Mexico and Central America, it will certainly make for a good contrast to other regions. Diving in the area is popular, either off the coast of Isla Mujeres or Cozumel, or in the underwater caves or cenotes found in the region. The Maya ruins of Tulum are gloriously located, and the quieter spot of Cobá is worth a trip, as is the wilderness reserve of Sian Ka'an. To the far south, Chetumal seems a world away from the tourist hot spots, but it is the stepping-off point for travel to Belize and Guatemala.

Isla Holbox → *Phone code: 984.*

Also north of Valladolid, but in the neighbouring state of Quintana Roo, turn off the road to Puerto Juárez after Nuevo Xcan to Isla Holbox. Buses to **Chiquilá** for boats, three times a day; also direct from Tizimín at 1130, connecting with the ferry, US$2.20. The ferry leaves for Holbox 0600 and 1430, one hour, US$1, returning to Chiquilá at 0500 and 1300. A bus to Mérida connects with the 0500 return ferry. If you miss the ferry a fisherman will probably take you (for about US$14). You can leave your car in the care of the harbour master for a small charge; his house is east of the dock. Take water with you if possible. During 'El Norte' season, the water is turbid and the beach is littered with seaweed.

There are five more uninhabited islands beyond Holbox. Beware of sharks and barracuda, although very few nasty occurrences have been reported. Off the rough and mostly unpopulated bulge of the Yucatán coastline are several islands, once notorious for contraband. Beware of mosquitoes in the area.

Cancún → *For listings, see pages 79-100. Phone code: 998.*

In 1970, when Cancún was 'discovered' by the Mexican tourist board, it was an inaccessible strip of barren land with beautiful beaches; the only road went straight past Cancún to Puerto Juárez for the ferry to Isla Mujeres, which had been a national tourist destination since the 1950s. Massive international investment and government sponsorship saw the luxury resort of Cancún completed within 25 years. The 25-km hotel zone, set on a narrow strip of land in the shape of a number seven alongside the coast, is an ultra-modern American-style boulevard, with five-star hotels, high-tech nightclubs, high-class shopping malls and branches of McDonald's, Burger King and Planet Hollywood.

Love or hate Cancún, its presence on the international tourism market is indisputable. From all-in-one package tours to international government conferences, Cancún has an enviable record. It's worth a trip just to see what it's like. Jump on a Ruta 1 or Ruta 2 bus and you'll quickly see the international hotel chains with hundreds of rooms, packed along the sinuous sand bar. Spotted along the way Hotel Zone international shopping brands, restaurants and entertainment centres provide the complete holiday experience. All this is the more impressive given that the area has had to cope with some of the worst hurricanes of the century as well as incidents of drug violence. Fortunately for the region's economy, the violence is never directed at (or usually even on the radar screens of) tourists, but take their toll instead on the local population, generally in the most isolated areas.

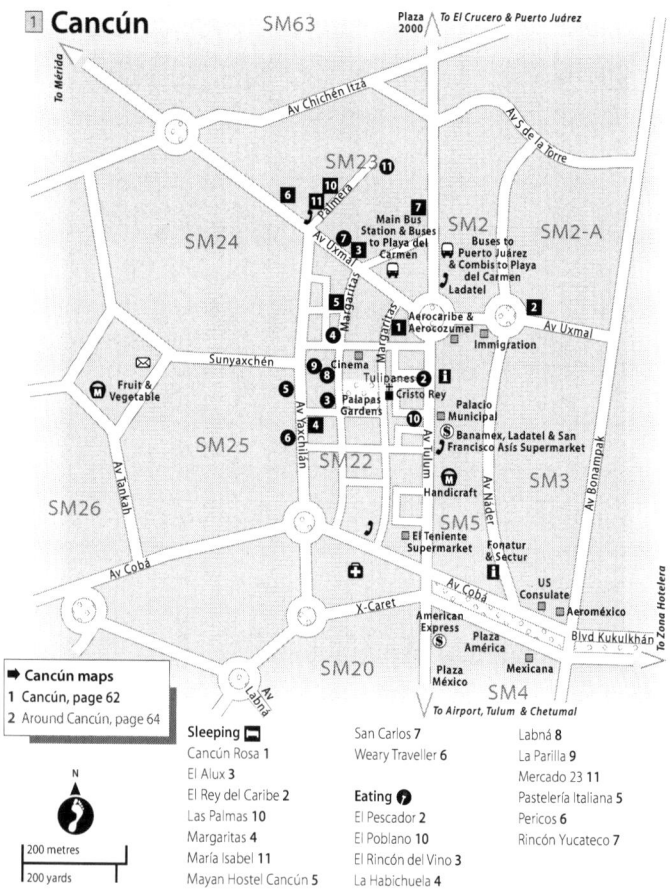

1 Cancún

→ Cancún maps
1 Cancún, page 62
2 Around Cancún, page 64

N
200 metres
200 yards

Sleeping
Cancún Rosa 1
El Alux 3
El Rey del Caribe 2
Las Palmas 10
Margaritas 4
María Isabel 11
Mayan Hostel Cancún 5

San Carlos 7
Weary Traveller 6

Eating
El Pescador 2
El Poblano 10
El Rincón del Vino 3
La Habichuela 4

Labná 8
La Parilla 9
Mercado 23 11
Pastelería Italiana 5
Pericos 6
Rincón Yucateco 7

Ins and outs

Getting there Cancún airport, www.cancun-airport.com, is 16 km south of the city. A fixed price *colectivo* taxi to the **Hotel Zone** or the centre costs US$9; pay at the kiosk outside airport. Drivers go via the Hotel Zone, but must take you to whichever part of the city centre you want. If going to the centre, make sure you know the name and address of your hotel before you get in the taxi, or the driver may offer to take you to a budget hotel of his own choice. ADO shuttle buses go to the centre via Avenida Tulum every 30 minutes from the airport. There is a tourist information kiosk in the airport, and a *casa de cambio*.

Getting around Ruta 1 and Ruta 2 buses go from the centre to the Hotel Zone, US$0.60; Ruta 1 runs 24 hours and goes via Avenida Tulum; Ruta 2 runs 0500-0330 and goes via Avenida Cobá to the bus terminal. Buses to the Hotel Zone can be caught from many stops along Avenida Tulum. Buses to **Puerto Juárez** for the boat to Isla Mujeres leave from outside **Cinema Royal**, across Avenida Tulum from the bus terminal, US$0.55. To get around in the centre, board a bus at Plaza 2000 and ask the driver if he's going to Mercado 28; those buses go along Avenida Yaxchilán; all others go to the Hotel Zone. Taxis are cheap and abundant in Cancún. Flat rate for anywhere within the centre is US$1.50; Hotel Zone from centre US$10-20. Many taxis stop at **El Crucero**, the junction of Avenida Tulum and Avenida López Portillo outside Plaza 2000, but there are often queues.

Downtown Cancún is a world apart from the Hotel Zone. It evolved from temporary shacks housing the thousands of builders working on the Hotel Zone, and is now a massive city with very little character. The main avenue is Tulum, formerly the highway running through the city when it was first conceived. It is now the location of the handicraft market, the main shops, banks and the municipal tourist office. There are also restaurants, but the better ones are along Avenida Yaxchilán, which is also the main centre for nightlife.

The cheaper end of the city, and a good area for budget travellers to base themselves, is around **El Crucero** (see above). The rest of the city is fairly expensive, but not as much as the Hotel Zone. The city is laid out in *supermanzanas* (SM), the blocks of streets between avenues, with smaller *manzanas* (M), or blocks, within them. Often the address you are given is, for example, SM24, M6, L3. L stands for *lote*, and is the precise number of the building within its *manzana*. This can lead to confusion when walking about, as the streets also have names, often not mentioned in the addresses. Look closely at street signs and you will see the SM and the M numbers. Taxi drivers generally respond better to addresses based on the *manzana* system.

Tourist information The **tourist office** ⓘ *Av Tulum 26, www.qroo.gob.mx, in a building that also houses local government offices*, is not very helpful; you'll get a glossy pocket guide to Cancún full of adverts for expensive restaurants and even more expensive hotels. There is a newer and well-equipped office at the **Conventions and Visitor Bureau** ⓘ *corner of Av Cobá and Av Bonampak, T884-6531*. Here the staff are helpful and friendly with information on new attractions, hotels and excursions.

Cancún to Isla Mujeres

A strip of coastline north of **Punta Sam** is officially part of Isla Mujeres. It is being developed as a luxury resort, but without the high-rise buildings of Cancún's Hotel Zone.

Puerto Juárez, about 3 km north of Cancún, is the dock for the cheaper ferry services to Isla Mujeres; there is also a bus terminal, but services are more frequent from Cancún. There are many buses between Cancún and Puerto Juárez, for example No 8 opposite the bus terminal (US$0.70). A taxi from Puerto Juárez to Downtown Cancún should be no more than US$2.

Isla Mujeres → *For listings, see pages 79-100. Phone code: 998.*

A refreshing antidote to the urban sprawl of Cancún, Isla Mujeres is a good place to relax for a few days away from the hurly-burly of package tourism. The island is especially nice in the evening, when all the Cancún day trippers have gone. The town is strictly low-rise, with brightly coloured buildings giving it a Caribbean island feel. The island's laws prohibit the construction of any building higher than three floors, and US franchises such as McDonald's and Walmart are not allowed to open branches here.

② Around Cancún

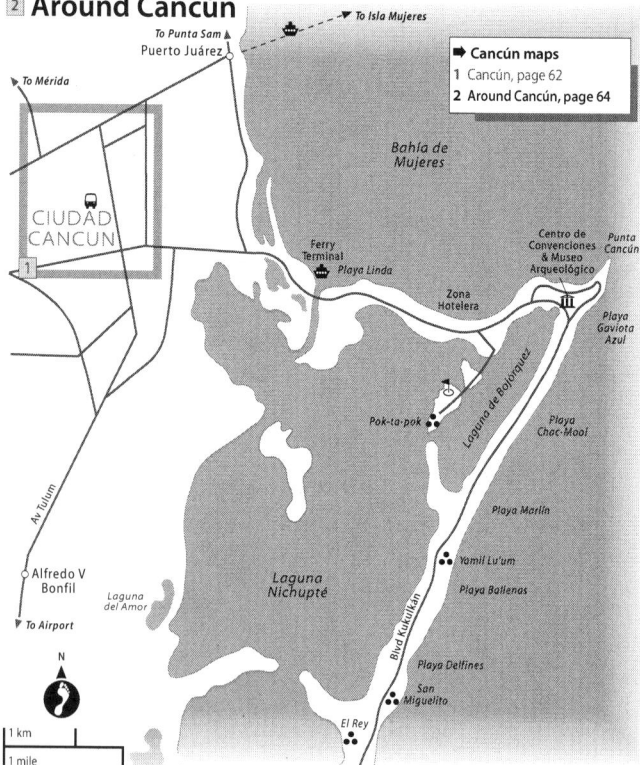

➡ Cancún maps
1 Cancún, page 62
2 Around Cancún, page 64

There are several good beaches on Isla Mujeres, the best being **Playa Cocos** on the northwest coast, five minutes' walk from the town. Further south, there are several places to swim, snorkel and observe marine life. Restaurants and nightspots are plentiful, good quality and cheaper than those on the mainland, and the people are friendlier. There are several ways to explore the island: you can rent a golf cart, many of which chug around the streets all day, good for families; mopeds and bicycles are cheap and plentiful to rent, and a public bus runs all the way from the town to El Paraíso, almost at the southern tip of the island.

The name Isla Mujeres refers to the large number of clay female idols found by the Spaniards here in 1518. The island contains the only known Maya shrine to a female deity: Ixchel, goddess of the moon and fertility. The ruins of the shrine are at the southern tip of the island. The **tourist office** ① *Rueda Medina, opposite the ferry dock, Mon-Fri 0900-1600, Sat-Sun 0900-1400, www.isla-mujeres.com.mx*, is very helpful. The immigration office is next door.

In October there is a festival of music, with groups from Mexico and the US performing in the main square, and from 1-12 December, during the fiesta for the Virgin of Guadalupe, there are fireworks and dances until 0400 in the plaza.

Sights

Most of the sights south of the town can be seen in a day. The first of these, 5 km from the town, is the **Turtle Farm** ① *daily 0900-1700, US$2*, with hundreds of sea turtles weighing from 170 g to 270 kg in a humane setting. To get there, take the bus to the final stop, Playa Paraíso, double back and walk five minutes along the main road.

At the centre of the island are the curious remains of a pirate's domain, called **Hacienda Mundaca** ① *daily 0900-1700, US$2*. A big, arch gate marks its entrance. Paths have been laid out among the large trees, but all that remains of the estate (called Vista Alegre) are one small building and a circular garden with raised beds, a well and a gateway. Fermín Mundaca, more of a slave-trader than a buccaneer, built Vista Alegre for the teenage girl he loved. She rejected him and he died, broken-hearted, in Mérida. His epitaph there reads *Como eres, yo fui; como soy, tu serás* ('As you are I was; as I am you shall be'). See the poignant little carving on the garden side of the gate, *La entrada de La Trigueña* (the girl's nickname). To get there, get off the bus at the final stop, and turn the opposite way to the beach; the house is a short walk away.

El Garrafón ① *T998-877 1100, www.garrafon.com*, is a snorkelling centre 7 km from the town, being developed into a luxury resort in the style of Xcaret on the mainland. Snorkelling is still possible, with a 12-m bronze cross submerged offshore for your exploration; by tour only. There is an expensive restaurant and bar at El Garrafón, and a small beach. The snorkelling is good past the pier, along a reef with some dead coral. Large numbers of different coloured fish can be seen at very close range. If you want to walk to El Garrafón from the bus stop at Playa Paraíso, take the second path on the right to the beach from the main road. The first path leads through **Restaurant Playa Paraíso**, which charges US$1 for the privilege of walking through their premises to the beach. Once on the beach, you can walk all the way to El Garrafón along the coast, although it gets very rocky for the final part. It is easier to go as far as the cluster of beach villas, then cut through one of them (ask for permission) to the main road. The whole walk takes about half an hour. When you arrive at El Garrafón, turn right at the building site, go down the hill to **Hotel Garrafón** del Castillo, which is the entrance to the snorkelling centre.

A further 15 minutes' walk from El Garrafón, at the tip of the island, are the ruins of the Maya shrine **Santuario Maya a la Diosa Ixchel**, US$2, dedicated to Ixchel the goddess of fertility. These were once free to visit, but unfortunately they have been bought and developed as part of the **El Garrafón 'National Park'** ⓘ *US$5.50*. A cultural centre has also been built here with large sculptures by several international artists.

South of Cancún → *For listings, see pages 79-100.*

Puerto Morelos → *Phone code: 998.*
A quiet little village 34 km south of Cancún, Puerto Morelos is one of the few places that still retains some of the charm of an unspoilt fishing village (but not for much longer), making it a good place to stop over en route to larger towns further south, such as Playa del Carmen. The village is really just a large plaza right on the seafront with a couple of streets going off it. If on arrival at Cancún airport you don't wish to spend the night in the city, you could get a taxi directly to Puerto Morelos. This is also the place to catch the car ferry to the island of Cozumel (see below). The **Sinaltur** office on the plaza offers a range of good snorkelling, kayak and fishing trips. **Goyos**, just north of the plaza, offers jungle adventures and rooms for rent, although erratic hours are maintained.

Playa del Carmen → *Phone code: 984.*
What used to be a pleasant little town on the beach has lost the charms of its former existence as a fishing village. Recent development for tourism has been rapid, but Playa, as it is known locally, has not had the high-rise treatment of Cancún. The beach is dazzling white, with crystal-clear shallow water, ideal for swimming, and further out there is good scuba-diving. There is lodging for every budget, and plenty of good restaurants and bars of every type. Many travellers choose Playa as their base for trips to the ruins of Tulum in the south, and archaeological sites such as Cobá in the interior.

The town is laid out in a grid system, with the main centre of tourist activity based on Avenida 5 (pedestrianized in the central section at night between 1800 and 0200), one block from and parallel with the beach. This is where the more expensive hotels and restaurants are, as well as being the centre for nightlife. Cheaper accommodation can be found up Avenida Juárez and further north of the beach.

Tourist information is scant, although there is a **tourism office** ⓘ *corner of Av Juárez and Av 15, T984-873 2804*, which has useful information and maps, and the kiosk on the main plaza will provide a copy of *Destination Playa del Carmen,* a useful guide with maps produced by US residents.

Playa del Carmen

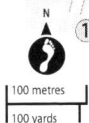

Sleeping
Alhambra **1** B4
Casa Tucán **5** B3
Cielo & El Carboncito
  Restaurant **7** B3
Happy Gecko **4** A3
Hostel Playa **8** A2
Las Molcas **6** D3
Mom's **11** B2
Posada Marinelly **13** C2
Tides Riviera Maya **2** A1
Urban Hostel **14** B3

Eating
Billy the Kid **1** B2
Buenos Aires **6** B3
El Fogón **8** A2
Glass Bar **12** A4
Habita Bookshop &
  Café **18** A4
Java Joe's **2** A4
Karen's **9** C3
La Parrilla **11** A4
Los Comales **10** B3
Maktub **22** A4
Pez Vela **5** C3
Rolandi **4** D3
Sushi-Tlan **23** A4
Tortas del Carmen **3** B2
Yaxche **7** A3

Bars & clubs
Beer Bucket **13** A3
Blue Parrot Inn **21** A4
Carlos 'n' Charlies **19** D3
Coco Maya **16** A4
El Cielo **17** A4
Habibi & Los
  Aguachiles **24** A4
OM **15** A4
Señor Frog's **20** D3
Tequila Barrel **14** A4

Cozumel → *For listings, see pages 79-100. Phone code: 987.*

The town, properly San Miguel de Cozumel, but always shortened to Cozumel, is a seedy, overpriced version of Playa del Carmen. Daily tour groups arrive on cruises from Miami and Cancún, and the town's services seem geared towards this type of tourist. But Cozumel is a mecca for scuba divers, with many beautiful offshore reefs to explore, as well as much interesting wildlife and birdlife. Travellers looking for a beach holiday with some nightlife will find the island disappointing compared to Playa del Carmen. There is only one nice beach on the west side, and the eastern, Atlantic coast is far too rugged and choppy for swimming.

1 Cozumel

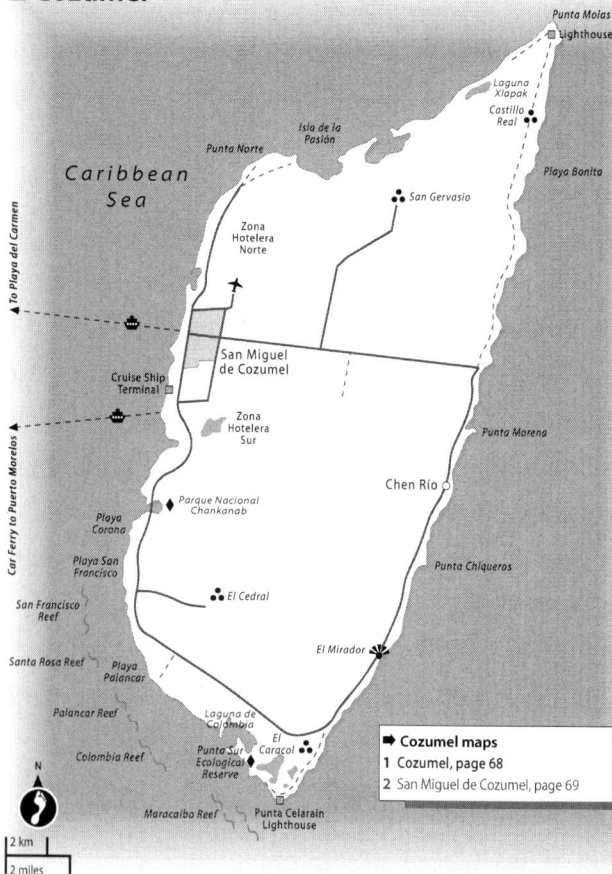

→ **Cozumel maps**
1 Cozumel, page 68
2 San Miguel de Cozumel, page 69

Ins and outs

The airport is just north of Cozumel with a minibus shuttle service to the hotels. There are 10-minute flights to and from the airstrip near Playa del Carmen, as well as flights linking to Mexico City, Cancún, Chichén Itzá and Houston (Texas). The passenger ferry from Playa del Carmen runs every two hours, and the car ferry leaves twice daily from Puerto Morelos (see page 66). There are no local buses, but Cozumel town is small enough to visit on foot. To get around the island, there are organized tours or taxis; otherwise, hire a jeep, moped or bicycle.

San Miguel de Cozumel

The island's only town has very little character, mainly due to the construction of a US air base during the Second World War, whose airfield has now been converted for civilian use. There is a variety of accommodation, with a few budget hotels, but mainly focusing on the luxury end of the market.

On the waterfront between Calle 4 and 6, the **Museo de la Isla** ① US$3.30, provides a well-laid-out history of the island. There is a bookshop, art gallery and rooftop restaurant,

② San Miguel de Cozumel

To ⑥ & Northern Hotel Sector

To Airport

Cozumel Channel

Av Rafael Melgar

Museo de la Isla

Av 5 Norte

Av 10 Norte

Calle 6 Norte

⑧ Av 15 Norte

Av 20 Norte

⑩ Av 25 Norte

Calle 4 Norte

Flea Market

④ Calle 2 Norte

Av Benito Juárez

Pemex

To San Gervasio & Caribbean Coast

Av Lic Pedro Joaquín Coldwell

Passenger Ferry

Taxis

Main Plaza

Catholic

Calle 1 Sur

Market & Loncherias

⑤

Av 20 Sur

Av 25 Sur

Calle Dr Adolfo Rosado Salas

⑦

Av 5 Sur

Av 10 Sur

Av 15 Sur

Calle 3 Sur

To ⑦, Post Office, Southern Hotel Sector,
Cruise Ship Terminal, Car Ferry Dock,
Playa San Francisco & Puerto Langosta

To ①

➡ **Cozumel maps**
1 Cozumel, page 68
2 San Miguel de Cozumel, page 69

N

100 metres
100 yards

Sleeping
Amaranto **1**
Flamingo **2**
Flores **3**
Pepita **5**
Posada Edén **4**

Posada Marruang **7**
Posada Zuanayoli **8**
Tamarindo **10**

Eating
Casa Deni's **3**

Casa Mission **1**
La Choza **5**
Las Palmeras **4**
Lobster's Cove **7**
Pancho's Backyard **6**
Prima **2**

which has excellent food and views of sunset, good for breakfast, from 0700 (**The Quick** is excellent value). Recommended.

Beaches
In the north of the island the beaches are sandy and wide, although those at the Zona Hotelera Norte were damaged in 1989 and again in 2005 and are smaller than they used to be. At the end of the paved road, walk up the unmade road until it becomes 'dual carriageway'; turn left for the narrow beach, which is a bit dirty. Cleaner beaches are accessible only through the hotels. South of San Miguel, **San Francisco** is good if narrow (clean, very popular, lockers at **Pancho's**, expensive restaurants), but others are generally narrower still and rockier.

All the main hotels are on the sheltered west coast. The east, Caribbean coast is rockier, but very picturesque; swimming and diving on the unprotected side is very dangerous owing to ocean underflows. The only safe place is at a sheltered bay at **Chen Río**. Another bay with possibilities is **Punta Morena**, which is a good surf beach, there is good accommodation (contact Matt at **Deep Blue**, on Salas 200, for more information and transport) and seafood (try the *ceviche*). Three good (and free) places for snorkelling are: the beach in front of **Hotel Las Glorias**, 15 minutes' walk south from ferry (you can walk through the hotel's reception); **Playa Corona**, further south, is too far to walk, so hitch or take a taxi (there is a small restaurant and pier); and **Xul-Ha**, further south still, which has a bar and comfortable beach chairs.

Archaeological sites
There are some 32 archaeological sites on Cozumel; those on the east coast are mostly single buildings (thought to have been lookouts, navigational aids). The easiest to see are the restored ruins of the Maya-Toltec period at **San Gervasio** ① *0900-1800, US$6, guides are on hand, or you can buy a self-guiding booklet at the bookshop on the square in San Miguel, or at the flea market, for US$1*. It is in the north of the island (7 km from Cozumel town, then 6 km to the left up a paved road, toll US$1), an interesting site, quite spread out, with *sacbés* (sacred roads) between the groups of buildings. There are no large structures, but a nice plaza, an arch, and pigment can be seen in places. It is also a pleasant place to listen to birdsong, see butterflies, animals (if lucky), lizards, land crabs and insects. **Castillo Real** is one of many sites on the northeastern coast, but the road to this part of the island is in very bad condition and the ruins themselves are very small. **El Cedral** in the southwest (3 km from the main island road) is a two-room temple, overgrown with trees, in the centre of the village of the same name. Behind the temple is a ruin, and next to it a modern church with a green and white façade (an incongruous pairing). In the village are large, permanent shelters for agricultural shows, rug sellers and locals who pose with *iguanas doradas* (golden iguanas). **El Caracol**, where the sun, in the form of a shell, was worshipped, is 1 km from the southernmost Punta Celarain. At Punta Celarain is an old lighthouse.

Around the island
A circuit of the island on paved roads can easily be done in a day. Head due east out of San Miguel (take the continuation of Avenida Juárez). Make the detour to San Gervasio before continuing to the Caribbean coast at **Mescalito's** restaurant. Here, turn left for the

Sweating it out

The temazcal is a ritual ceremony that has been practised by the indigenous peoples of Mexico for hundreds of years. The Mexican version of the sweat lodge, it is a thanksgiving to the four elements, and a healing for the spirit as well as the body. You enter the womb of mother earth when you enter the temazcal, and when you exit you are born a new being. Traditionally, it was done in a square or dome-shaped building constructed from branches and then covered with blankets, and was preceded by a day of fasting. There are temazcal sessions open to newcomers all over Mexico. Done properly, the experience can be very intense.

Red-hot rocks are placed in the centre of the construction, and a group sits around them. The door is closed, and a medicine man leads the group in prayer and songs, all designed to connect the insiders to each of the four elements. During the ceremony, the door is opened four times, to allow people who want to leave (there is no returning), and to bring in more hot rocks. Different emotions and thoughts come up for different people, and everyone is encouraged to contribute something from their own traditions if they feel the need. After each contribution, herbal water is poured over the rocks to create more healing steam. This continues till everyone is in agreement to open the fourth and final door. Everyone then leaves, rinses off (hopefully in the sea or lagoon if you're near the coast), then shares soup and tea to break their fast.

northern tip (road unsuitable for ordinary vehicles), or right for the south, passing Punta Morena, Chen Río, Punta Chiqueros (restaurant, bathing), El Mirador (a low viewpoint with sea-worn rocks, look out for holes) and Paradise Cove. At this point, the paved road heads west while an unpaved road continues south to Punta Celarain. Here there is the **Punta Sur Ecological Reserve** ① *T987-872 0914, www.cozumelparks.com.mx, 1000-1700, US$10*, an ecotourism development, with a variety of natural landscapes with lagoons and mangrove jungles. A snorkelling centre has opened here as well as a viewing platform. On the road west, opposite the turn-off to El Cedral, is a sign to **Restaurante Mac y Cía**, an excellent fish restaurant on a lovely beach, popular with dive groups for lunch. Next is Playa San Francisco (see above). A few more kilometres leads to the former Holiday Inn, the last big hotel south of San Miguel.

Just after this is **Parque Chankanab** ① *0800-1800, US$16, snorkelling mask and fins US$5, use of underwater camera US$25*, which used to be an idyllic lagoon behind the beach (9 km from San Miguel). After it became totally spoilt, it was restored as a national park, with the lagoon, crystal clear again, a botanical garden with local and imported plants, a 'Maya Area' (rather artificial), swimming (ideal for families with young children), snorkelling, dive shops, souvenirs, expensive but good restaurants and lockers (US$2). Soon the road enters the southern Hotel Zone at the **Stouffer Presidente**, coming to the cruise ship dock and car ferry port on the outskirts of town.

South of Playa del Carmen → *For listings, see pages 79-100.*

The Maya site of **Xcaret** ⓘ *T01-800-292-2738, www.xcaret.com, US$59 adults, under 5s free*, an ancient port called Polé, was the departure point for voyages to Cozumel. It has now been turned into an overpriced and very tacky theme park catering exclusively for day-trippers. There is a 1-km walk from the entrance to Xcaret. The alternative is to take a taxi, or a tour from Playa del Carmen or Cancún (in a multicoloured bus). You can also walk along the beach from Playa del Carmen (three hours).

A luxury resort, 102 km south of Cancún, 20 km north of Tulum, **Akumal** is reached easily by bus from there or from Playa del Carmen (30 minutes). There is a small lagoon 3 km north of Akumal, with good snorkelling. The coastline from Playa del Carmen down to just short of Tulum to the south is known as the 'Riviera Maya' – a strip of upmarket, generally all-inclusive hotels. Two ferries run daily to Cozumel. Also just south of Akumal are **Chemuyil** (palapas for hammocks, US$4, free shower, expensive restaurant, laundry facilities) and **Xcacel** (campground has water, bathrooms, cold showers and restaurant, very clean, US$2 per person, vehicles free, snorkel hire US$5 a day, beautiful swimming in the bay). Ask guards if you can go on turtle protection patrol at night (May to July).

Thirteen kilometres north of Tulum, 122 km from Cancún (bus from Playa del Carmen, 45 minutes), the beautiful clear lagoon of **Laguna Xel-Há** ⓘ *daily 0800-1630, US$10*, is full of fish, but fishing is not allowed as it is a national park. Snorkelling gear can be rented at US$7 for a day, but it is often in poor repair; better to rent from your hotel. Lockers cost US$1.50. Arrive as early as possible to see fish as the lagoon is full of tourists throughout most of the day. Snorkelling areas are limited by fencing. Bungalows, first-class hotels and fast-food restaurants are being built. The food and drink is very expensive. There is a marvellous jungle path to one of the lagoon bays. Xel-Há ruins, known also as **Los Basadres** ⓘ *US$3.35*, are located across the road from the beach of the same name. Few tourists but not much to see. You may have to jump the fence to visit; there is a beautiful *cenote* at the end of the ruins where you can have a lovely swim.

Tulum → *Phone code: 984.*
ⓘ *Daily 0800-1800, entry US$4.50, parking US$1.50, students with Mexican ID free.*
The Maya-Toltec ruins of Tulum are perched on coastal cliffs in a beautiful setting above the azure sea. The ruins are 12th century, with city walls of white stone. The temples were dedicated to the worship of the Falling God, or the Setting Sun, represented as a falling character over nearly all west-facing doors (Cozumel was the home of the Rising Sun). The same idea is reflected in the buildings, which are wider at the top than at the bottom.

The main structure is the **Castillo**, which commands a view of both the sea and the forested Quintana Roo lowlands stretching westwards. All the Castillo's openings face west, as do most, but not all, of the doorways at Tulum. Look for the alignment of the **Falling God** on the temple of that name (to the left of the Castillo) with the pillar and the back door in the **House of the Chultún** (the nearest building in the centre group to the entrance). The majority of the main structures are roped off so that you cannot climb the Castillo, nor get close to the surviving frescoes, especially on the **Temple of the Frescoes**.

Tulum is crowded with tourists (best time to visit is between 0800 and 0900). Take towel and swimsuit if you wish to scramble down from the ruins to one of the two beaches for a swim (the larger of the two is less easy to get to). The reef is from 600 m to

Tulum to Chetumal

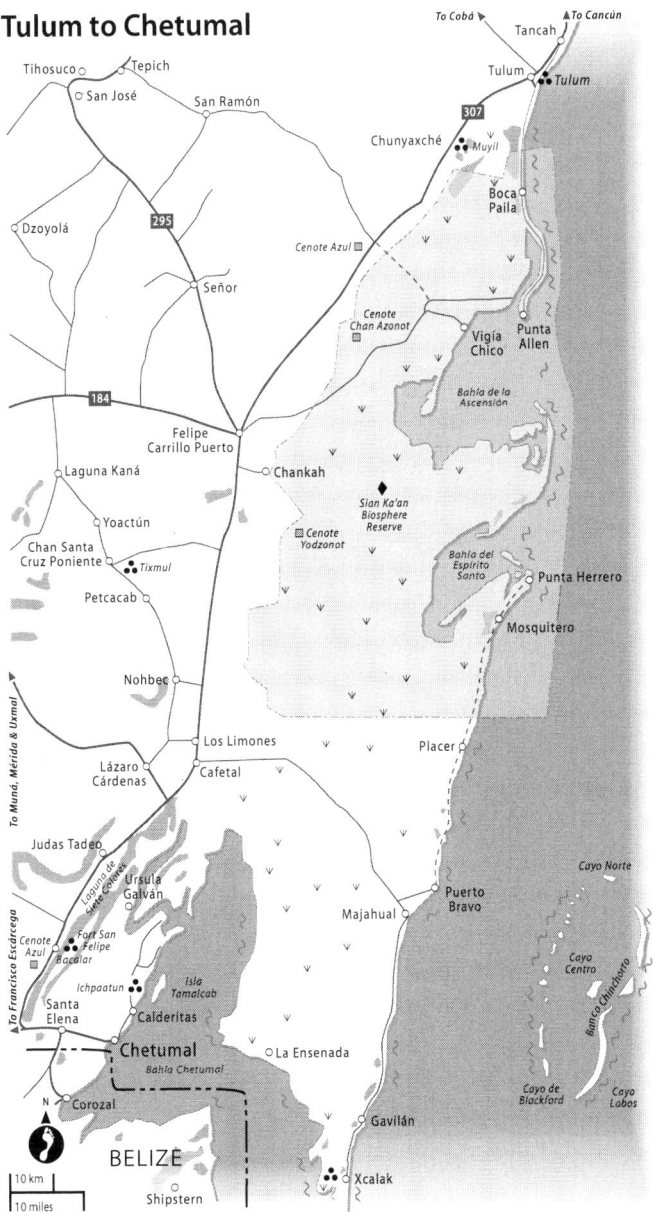

To Cobá
To Cancún
Tancah

Tihosuco
Tepich
San José
San Ramón
Tulum
Tulum

307
Chunyaxché
Muyil

Boca
Paila

Dzoyolá

295

Señor

Cenote Azul

Cenote
Chan Azanot
Vigía
Chico
Punta
Allen

184

Bahía de la
Ascensión

Felipe
Carrillo Puerto
Chankah

Laguna Kaná

Sian Ka'an
Biosphere
Reserve

Yoactún

Cenote
Yodzonot

Chan Santa
Cruz Poniente
Tixmul

Bahía del
Espíritu
Santo
Punta Herrero

Petcacab

Mosquitero

Nohbec

Los Limones
Placer

Lázaro
Cárdenas
Cafetal

To Muná, Mérida & Uxmal

Judas Tadeo

Laguna de Siete Colores

Cayo Norte

Ursula
Galván

Majahual
Puerto
Bravo

Cenote
Azul
Fort San
Felipe
Bacalar

Cayo
Centro

Bahía Chinchorro

Ichpaatun
Isla
Tamalcab

To Francisco Escárcega

Santa
Elena
Calderitas

Chetumal
Bahía Chetumal
La Ensenada

Cayo de
Blackford
Cayo
Lobos

N

Corozal

BELIZE

Gavilán

10 km
10 miles

Xcalak

Shipstern

1000 m from the shore, so if you wish to snorkel you must either be a strong swimmer, or take a boat trip.

There is a tourist complex at the entrance to the ruins. Guide books can be bought in the shops, local guides can also be hired. About two hours are needed to view at leisure. The parking area is near Highway 307, and there's a handicraft market. A small train takes you from the parking area to the ruins for US$2, or it is an easy 500 m walk. The paved road continues down the coast to **Boca Paila** and beyond, access by car to this road from the car park is closed. To reach the road south of the ruins, access is possible 1 km from Tulum village. Public buses drop passengers at El Crucero, a crossroads 500 m north of the car park for Tulum Ruinas (an easy walk) where there is an ADO bus terminal that is open for a few hours from 0800; at the crossroads are some hotels, a shop (will exchange traveller's cheques), on the opposite side of the road a naval base and airstrip, and a little way down Highway 307 a Pemex station.

If staying in the area, the beach running south of the ruins is dotted with quiet, isolated *palapas*, *cabañas* and hotels to fit most budgets. Alternatively the village of **Tulum** (as opposed to the ruins) is 4 km south of El Crucero. A taxi from the village to the ruins costs US$3. It is not very large but is growing rapidly and has a bus station, post office, bank (HSBC), several grocery shops, two bakeries, hotels and restaurants. There is a **tourist information office** in the village, next to the police station, two blocks north of the bus terminal. The information centre set up by the *Weary Traveller* backpacker centre has taken over as the primary source of information for this area. Located at the southern end of town a block away from the ADO bus terminal. Friendly and knowledgeable staff give fairly impartial information on hotels, excursions and restaurants. Another source of information is the **Sian Ka'an Information Centre** ① *Av Tulum between Satélite and Géminis, Tulum, T984-871 2363, siankaan_tours@hotmail.com*, which has information about visiting the reserve (see below) and several other areas of interest.

Cobá → *Phone code: 985.*
① *Daily 0800-1700, US$4.50.*
An important Maya city in the eighth and ninth centuries AD, whose population is estimated to have been between 40,000 and 50,000, Cobá was abandoned for unknown reasons. The present-day village of Cobá lies on either side of Lago Cobá, surrounded by dense jungle, 47 km inland from Tulum. It is a quiet, friendly village, with few tourists staying overnight.

The entrance to the ruins of this large but little-excavated city is at the end of the lake between the two parts of the village. A second lake, **Lago Macanxoc**, is within the site. There are turtles and many fish in the lakes. It is a good birdwatching area. Both lakes and their surrounding forest can be seen from the summit of the **Iglesia**, the tallest structure in the **Cobá Group**. There are three other groups of buildings to visit: the **Macanxoc Group**, mainly stelae, about 1.5 km from the Cobá Group; **Las Pinturas**, 1 km northeast of Macanxoc, with a temple and the remains of other buildings that had columns in their construction; the **Nohoch Mul Group**, at least another kilometre from Las Pinturas. Nohoch Mul has the tallest pyramid in the northern Yucatán, a magnificent structure, from which the views of the jungle on all sides are superb. You will not find at Cobá the great array of buildings that can be seen at Chichén Itzá or Uxmal, or the compactness of Tulum. Instead, the delight of the place is the architecture in the jungle, with birds, butterflies, spiders and lizards, and the many uncovered structures that hint at the vastness of the city in its heyday (the urban extension of Cobá is put at some 70 sq km). An unusual feature is the network of *sacbés* (sacred roads), which connect the groups in the site and are known to have extended across the entire Maya Yucatán. Over 40 *sacbés* pass through Cobá, some local, some of great length, such as the 100-km road to Yaxuná in Yucatán state.

At the lake, toucans may be seen very early; also look out for greenish-blue and brown mot-mots in the early morning. The guards at the site are very strict about opening and closing time so it is hard to get in to see the dawn or sunset from a temple.

The paved road into Cobá ends at **Lago Cobá**; to the left are the ruins, to the right **Villas Arqueológicas**. The roads around Cobá are badly potholed. Cobá is becoming more popular as a destination for tourist buses, which come in at 1030; arrive before that to avoid the crowds and the heat (ie on the 0430 bus from Valladolid, if not staying in Cobá). Take insect repellent.

Sian Ka'an Biosphere Reserve

① Daily 0900-1500, 1800-2000, US$2. For information, visit Los Amigos de Sian Ka'an in Cancún, T984-884 9583, www.amigosdesiankaan.org; very helpful.

This enormous reserve, the third-largest and one of the most diverse in all Mexico, was declared a UNESCO World Heritage Site in 1987 and now covers 652,000 ha (4500 sq km) of the Quintana Roo coast. About one-third is covered in tropical forest, one-third is savannah and mangrove and one-third coastal and marine habitats, including 110 km of barrier reef. Mammals include jaguar, puma, ocelot and other cats, monkeys, tapir, peccaries, manatee and deer; turtles nest on the beaches; there are crocodiles and a wide variety of land and aquatic birds. Do not try to get there independently without a car.

Ecocolors *① Cancún, T/F884-9580*, in collaboration with **Los Amigos**, run tours to the reserve, US$115 for a full day, starting at 0700, pick up at hotel, everything included; in winter the tour goes through a canal, in summer it goes birdwatching, in both cases a visit to a Maya ruin, a *cenote*, snorkelling, all equipment, breakfast and evening meal are included. Two-day camping trips can be arranged. Two-hour boat trips through the biosphere can be taken for US$75. Trips can also be arranged through **Cabañas Ana y José**, near Tulum (see page 84).

Another highly regarded non-profit outfit that perhaps does a better job than any is the **Centro Ecológico Sian Ka'an** *① Carretera Nacional Cancún–Tulum at Km 68 in Tulum, T984-871 2499, www.cesiak.org*. It is possible to drive into the reserve from Tulum village as far as Punta Allen (58 km; the road is opposite the turning to Cobá; it is not clearly marked, and the final section is badly potholed); beyond that you need a launch. From the south it is possible to drive to Punta Herrero (unmade road, see Mahahual, below).

Muyil

① US$4.

The ruins of Muyil at **Chunyaxché** three pyramids (partly overgrown) are on the left-hand side of the road towards Felipe Carrillo Puerto, 18 km south of Tulum. One of the pyramids is undergoing reconstruction; the other two are relatively untouched. They are very quiet, with interesting birdlife although they are mosquito infested. Beyond the last pyramid is Laguna Azul, which is good for swimming and snorkelling in blue, clean water (you do not have to pay to visit the pool if you do not visit the pyramids).

Cenote diving

There are more than 50 *cenotes* in this area – accessible from Ruta 307 and often well signposted – and cave diving has become very popular. However, it is a specialized sport and, unless you have a cave diving qualification, you must be accompanied by a qualified Dive Master.

A cave diving course involves over 12 hours of lectures and a minimum of 14 cave dives using double tanks, costing around US$600. Accompanied dives start at around US$60. Specialist dive centres offering courses are: Mike Madden's **CEDAM Dive Centres**, PO Box 1, Puerto Aventuras, T/F984-873 5129; **Aquatech**, Villas de Rosa, PO Box 25, T984-875 9020, www.cenotes.com. **Aventuras Akumal No 35**, Tulum, T984-875 9030; **Aktun Dive Centre**, PO Box 119, Tulum, T984-871 2311, and **Cenote Dive Center**, Tulum, T984-871 2232, www.cenote dive.com, Norwegian owned.

Two of the best *cenotes* are 'Carwash', on the Cobá road, good even for beginners, with excellent visibility; and 'Dos Ojos', just off Ruta 307 south of Aventuras, the second largest underground cave system in the world. It has a possible link to the Nohoch Nah Chich, the most famous *cenote* and part of a subterranean system recorded as the world's largest, with over 50 km of surveyed passageways connected to the sea.

A word of warning: *cenote* diving has a higher level of risk than open-water diving – do not take risks and only dive with recognized operators.

Felipe Carrillo Puerto

The cult of the 'talking cross' was founded here. The **Santuario de la Cruz Parlante** is five blocks west of the Pemex station on Highway 307. The beautiful main square, which has playground equipment for children, is dominated by the Catholic church, built by the Cruzob in the 19th century. Legend has it that the unfinished bell tower will only be completed when the descendants of those who heard the talking cross reassert control of the region.

Mahahual and around

Further south on Route 307, at Cafetal, a good road heads east to Mahahual (Majahual) on the coast (56 km from Cafetal), a peaceful, unspoilt place with clear water and beautiful beaches. The cruise ship dock gives a clue to the occasional interruption to the peace and calm with Mahahual welcoming cruise ships travelling up and down the Mexican and Central American coast. ADO buses leave from the main terminal in Chetumal at 0530 and 1930, returning at 0630 and 1830. An offshore excursion is possible to **Banco Chinchorro**, where there is a coral bank and a white-sand beach.

About 2 km before Mahahual a paved road to the left goes to **Puerto Bravo** and on to Placer and **Punta Herrero** (in the Sian Ka'an Biosphere Reserve, see above).

Just over 3 km along this road a right turn goes to the Sol y Mar restaurant, with rooms to rent, coconut palms and beach. Another 10.5 km along the Punta Herrero road, again on the right, is **Camidas Trailer Park**, see Sleeping, page 85.

Xcalak

Across the bay from Chetumal, at the very tip of Quintana Roo, is Xcalak, which may be reached from Chetumal by private launch (two hours), or by the unpaved road from Cafetal to Mahahual, then turning south for 55 km (186 km by road from Chetumal, suitable for passenger cars but needs skilled driver). *Colectivos* from Chetumal leave daily between 0700 and 1900 (16 de Septiembre 183 and Mahatma Ghandi); check return times. Buses run Friday 1600 and Sunday 0600, returning Saturday morning and Sunday afternoon (details from the Chetumal tourist office). Xcalak is a fishing village with a few shops selling beer and basic supplies and one small restaurant serving Mexican food. A few kilometres north of Xcalak are two hotels, Costa de Cocos and Villa Caracol, both American-run; the latter is good, with comfortable *cabañas*, although expensive (it has sport fishing and diving facilities). From here trips can be arranged to the unspoiled islands of Banco Chinchorro or to San Pedro, Belize. In the village you may be able to rent a boat to explore Chetumal Bay and Banco Chinchorro. Do not try to walk from Xcalak along the coast to San Pedro, Belize; the route is virtually impassable.

Chetumal

To Bus Station (16 blocks approx) at Av Insurgentes

To Calderitas

To Zoo, Bacalar, Francisco Escárcega, Kohunlich & Corozal (Belize)

Colón

Museo de la Cultura Maya

Francisco Primo de Verdad

Colectivo to Bacalar

Ghandi

ADO

Av Belice

Av Erain Aguilar

Héroes de Chapultepec

To Guatemalan Consulate

Independencia

Av Benito Juárez

Lázaro Cárdenas

Av Héroes

Av HEPE Calles

Zaragoza

16 de Septiembre

Obregón

Othón P Blanco

Carmen Ochoa de Merino

Palacio de Gobierno

22 de Enero

Boulevard Bahía

Calzada Veracruz

Av Miguel Hidalgo

Av Reforma

H Escuela Naval

Sagrado Corazón

Bahía de Chetumal

N

200 metres
200 yards

Sleeping 🛏
Caribe Princess 2
Cristal 3
El Dorado 4
Los Cocos 6

María Dolores 7
Real Azteca 8
Ucúm 10

Eating 🍴
El Emporio 2
El Fenicio 3
Los Milagros 4
Pantoja 5
Sergio Pizza 1

Chetumal → *For listings, see pages 79-100.*
Phone code: 983.

The state capital of Quintana Roo, Chetumal, is a necessary stopover for travellers en route to Maya sites in the south of the peninsula, and across the frontier to Belize and Guatemala. Although attractions are thin on the ground, Chetumal does have the advantage of being a small Mexican city not devoted to tourism, and thus has a more authentic feel than other towns on the Riviera Maya. It is also the logical spot for obtaining exit and entry visas. It is 240 km south of Tulum. The Chetumal bay has been designated a natural protected area for manatees, and includes a manatee sanctuary.

The avenues are broad, busy and in the centre lined with huge shops selling cheap imported goods. The main local activity is window-shopping, and the atmosphere is more like a North American city, with an impression of affluence that can be a culture shock to the visitor arriving from the much poorer country of Guatemala. The **tourist office** ① *on the main plaza, opposite the Museo de Cultura Maya, Mon-Fri 0900-1900, Sat 0900-1300*, is mainly for trade enquiries. There is very little tourist information in Chetumal; it is usually best to go to a travel agent such as **Tu-Maya** (see page 93).

The *paseo* near the waterfront on Sunday night is worth seeing. The State Congress building has a mural showing the history of Quintana Roo. The **Museo de la Cultura Maya** ① *Av Héroes de Chapultepec by the market, Tue-Sun 0900-1900, US$5*, is highly recommended. It has good models of sites and touch screen computers explaining the Maya calendar and glyphs. Although there are few original Maya pieces, it gives an excellent overview; some explanations are in English, guided tours are available, and there's a good bookshop with English magazines.

Around Chetumal → *For listings, see pages 79-100.*

Towards Bacalar

Six kilometres north of Chetumal are the stony beaches of **Calderitas**, bus every 30 minutes from Colón, between Belice and Héroes, US$1.80, or taxi US$5, many fish restaurants. There is camping at Calderitas, signposted, OK, US$2.75. Beyond are the unexcavated archaeological sites of **Ichpaatun** (13 km), **Oxtancah** (14 km) and **Nohochmul** (20 km). Sixteen kilometres north on Route 307 to Tulum is the **Laguna de los Milagros**, a beautiful lagoon for swimming. Further on, 34 km north of Chetumal, is **Cenote Azul**, over 70 m deep, with a waterside restaurant serving inexpensive and good seafood and regional food (but awful coffee) until 1800. Both the *laguna* and the *cenote* are deserted in the week.

About 3 km north of Cenote Azul is the village of **Bacalar** (nice, but not special) on the **Laguna de Siete Colores**, which has swimming and skin-diving; *colectivos* from terminal (Suchaa) in Chetumal, corner of Miguel Hidalgo and Primo de Verdad, 0700-1900 every 30 minutes, US$1.60, return from plaza when full; also buses from Chetumal bus station every two hours or so, US$1.60. There is a Spanish fort there overlooking a beautiful shallow, clear, freshwater lagoon, and abundant birdlife on the lake shore. This is the fort of **San Felipe**, said to have been built around 1729 by the Spanish to defend the area from the English pirates and smugglers of logwood. There is a plaque praying for protection from the British and a small **museum** ① *US$0.70*. The British ships roamed the islands and reefs, looting Spanish galleons laden with gold, on their way from Peru to Cuba. There are many old shipwrecks on the reef and around the Banco Chinchorro, 50 km out in the Caribbean (information kindly provided by Coral Pitkin of the **Rancho Encantado**, see page 85). There is a dock for swimming from north of the plaza, with a restaurant and disco next to it. North of Bacalar a direct road (Route 293) runs to Muná, on the road between Mérida and Uxmal. Gasoline is sold in a side-street.

Towards Francisco Villa

From Chetumal you can visit the fascinating Maya ruins that lie west on the way (Route 186) to Francisco Villa and Escárcega, if you have a car. There are few tourists in this area and few facilities. Take plenty of drinking water. About 25 km from Chetumal at **Ucum** (where fuel is available), you can turn off 5 km south to visit **Palmara**, located along the Río Hondo, which borders Belize; there are swimming holes and restaurant.

Just before Francisco Villa (61 km from Chetumal), the ruins of **Kohunlich** ① *0800-1700, US$3*, lie 8.5 km south of the main road, 1½ hours' walk along a sweltering, unshaded road; take plenty of water. Descriptions in Spanish and English. Every hour or so the van passes for staff working at **Explorer Kohunlich**, a luxury resort hotel halfway to the ruins, which may give you a lift, but you'll still have 4 km to walk. There are fabulous masks (early Classic, AD 250-500) set on the side of the main pyramid, still bearing red colouring; they are unique of their kind (allow an hour for the site). About 200 m west of the turning for Kohunlich is an immigration office and a stall selling beer; wait here for buses to Chetumal or Xpujil, which have to stop, but first-class buses will not pick up passengers. *Colectivos* 'Nicolás Bravo' from Chetumal, or bus marked 'Zoh Laguna' from bus station pass the turning.

Other ruins in this area are **Dzibanché** and **Knichná** ① *0900-1700, US$3*. Both are recent excavations and both are accessible down a dirt road off the Chetumal–Morocoy road. In the 1990s the remains of a Maya king were disinterred at Dzibanché, which is thought to have been the largest Maya city in southern Quintana Roo, peaking between AD 300 and 1200. Its discoverer, Thomas Gann, named it in 1927 after the Maya glyphs he found engraved on the sapodilla wood lintels in Temple VI – *Dzibanché* means 'writing on the wood' in Maya. Later excavations revealed a tomb in Temple I, believed to have belonged to a king because of the number of offerings it contained. This temple is also known as the **Temple of the Owl** because one of the artefacts unearthed was a vase and lid carved with an owl figure. Other important structures are the **Temple of the Cormorants** and **Structure XIII**, known as 'The Captives', due to its friezes depicting prisoners. Knichná means 'House of the Sun' in Maya, christened by Thomas Gann in reference to a glyph he found there. The **Acropolis** is the largest structure. To reach these sights follow the Chetumal-Escárcega road, turn off at Km 58 towards Morocoy, 9 km further on. The road to Dzibanché is 2 km down this road, crossing the turning for Knichná.

State of Quintana Roo listings

For Sleeping and Eating price codes and other relevant information, see pages 12-13.

● Sleeping

Isla Holbox *p61*
Holbox has almost exclusively high-end accommodation; what else remains is not recommended.
$$$ Faro Viejo, Av Juárez, on the beach, T984-875 2217, www.faroviejoholbox.com.mx. Large, breezy rooms looking over the beach. Some rooms with kitchens.
$$$ La Palapa, Av Morelos 231, T984-875 2121, www.hotellapalapa.com. Very clean cabins, leading onto the beach.
$$$ Mawimbi, T984-875 2003, www.mawimbi.com.mx. Stylishly decorated *cabañas* with kitchenette, stepping out onto the beach.

$$$ Villa Delfines, on the beach, T984-875 2196, www.villasdelfines.com. 20 romantic palm-roofed bungalows, leading onto the beach, pool, garden and bar, expensive but nice.
$$$ Villa Los Mapaches, Av Pedro Joaquín Coldwell s/n, on beach, T984-875 2090, www.losmapaches.com. Secluded, romantic cabins away from it all and fully furnished. Kitchenettes.

Camping
Best camping on beach east of village (north side of island).

Cancún *p61, maps p62 and p64*
Almost all accommodation – decent or otherwise – in the Hotel Zone now starts

at around US$100, rises quickly and is best arranged as part of a package holiday. The increased costs – already the highest in Mexico – are also the result of a government-mandated rebuilding drive after 2 devastating hurricanes required all existing hotels to upgrade structures for safety. The beaches are supposedly public so you don't have to stay in a hotel to hang out on the beach, although this is not advertised and meandering along the strand is not encouraged by the larger hotels. The centre or downtown area has many cheaper options, but prices are still higher than other parts of the Yucatán Peninsula.

Hotel Zone

Some of these hotels have special offers during Jul and Aug, listed in *Riviera Maya Hotels Guide*, available free at the airport. Discounts can be considerable here as with anywhere on the coast during low season. 2 good high-end options are:

$$$$ Le Meridien, Retorno del Rey Km 14, T998-881 2200, www.starwood hotels.com/lemeridien.

$$$$ Presidente Inter-Continental, Av Kukulcán Km 7.5, T998-848 8700, www.presidentecancun.com.

Town centre

Many hotels, especially the budget ones, tend to be full during Semana Santa and in Jul, and increasingly so over the Dec-Jan holidays. It is best to get to them as early as possible in the morning, or try to make a reservation if planning to return to Cancún after a trip to the interior or Isla Mujeres. Prices drop considerably in the low season. El Crucero, location of some of the budget hotels, is said by locals to be safe during the day, but unsafe at night.

$$$ El Rey del Caribe, Av Uxmal 24 and Náder, T998-884 2028, www.reycaribe.com. This hotel has clean, comfortable a/c rooms, some with cooker and fridge. There's a lush

garden slung with hammocks and the spa has interesting treatments, such as chocolate or honey and milk massage.

$$$ Margaritas, Yaxchilán 41 and Jasmines, T998-884 7870, www.margaritas cancun.com. A clean and modern hotel with a range of efficient services including restaurant, bar, car rental, laundry and pool. There are over 100 rooms, all with a/c, balcony and cable TV.

$$ Cancún Rosa, Margaritas 2, local 10, T998-884 0623. Located close to the bus terminal, this hotel has tidy rooms of various sizes (including family size), all with cable TV and a/c. Management is friendly.

$$ El Alux, Av Uxmal 21, T998-884 0556, www.hotelalux.com. Turn left and first right from bus station. Clean rooms with a/c and bath. Some are cheaper and good value. Beware of the persistent tout outside, trying to take you to a cheap hovel. Recommended.

$$-$ Las Palmas, Palmeras 43, T998-884 2513, www.hotel-laspalmascancun.com. This friendly family-run hotel has very clean, good-value rooms with cable TV and a/c, and they'll store luggage. Breakfast is included and there's a cheap dormitory too. Recommended.

$$-$ María Isabel, Palmera 59, T998-884 9015, hotelmariaisabelcancun@yahoo. com.mx, near bus station and Av Tulum. A small hotel with clean and relatively economical rooms, all with a/c and TV. Friendly and recommended, but can be noisy.

$$-$ Mayan Hostel Cancún, Margaritas 17 SM22, T998-892 0103, www.mayan hostel.com. Price per person. *Palapa*-style dorms, private rooms, fan or a/c, Breakfast, dinner and internet included in the price. Laundry and kitchen. Good service.

$$-$ San Carlos, Cedro 40 (5th turning onto Cedro from bus terminal), opposite Mercado 23, T998-884 0602, www.hotelsancarlo scancun.com, handy for the bus terminal. Mixed bag of rooms, with mixed tariffs. Some rooms are a bit noisy and smelly, the upper floor is OK and a bit cheaper, but beware of very rickety stairs.

$ Weary Traveller, Palmera 30, entrance in Av Uxmal, T998-887 0191, reservations@ wearytravelerhostel.com. Funky budget hostel with dormitories and private rooms (**$$**). There's free internet, breakfast included in the price, TV, lockers and chillout space.

Camping

A big trailer park has been built opposite Punta Sam, 150 spaces, camping (**$** per person), shop selling basic commodities. Irregular bus service there, or hitchhike from Puerto Juárez. Check to see if restaurant is open evenings. Take mosquito repellent.

Isla Mujeres *p64*

$$$$ Condominio Nautibeach, Playa Los Cocos, T998-877 0606, www.nautibeach.com. This hotel feels a bit like a giant warren, but has comfortable, a/c apartments and condos, right on the beach, facing the sunset. **Sunset Grill**, attached, is perfect for sundowners and there's a nice pool too.

$$$$-$$$ María del Mar, Av Carlos Larzo 1, on the road down to the north beach, T998-877 0179, www.cabanasdelmar.com. Good clean rooms and *cabañas*, close to the best beach. There's a restaurant, pool, beach bar, hammocks and a cool, tranquil garden for chilling out. Organizes fishing excursions and cultural tours.

$$$ Rocamar, Nicolás Bravo and Zona Marítima, T998-877 0101, www.rocamar-hotel.com. A large, well-established hotel, located on the quieter, eastern side of the island, where the sea is wilder and swimming not recommended. There's a range of rooms; the more expensive overlook the sea and the Caribbean sunrise and also have a jacuzzi.

$$ Hotel Bucaneros, Hidalgo 11, T998-877 1222, www.bucaneros.com. A pleasant, professionally managed hotel, right in the heart of town. It has 18 modern rooms, all

with calm, neutral interiors. There's a good restaurant attached.

$$-$ Hotel Carmelina, Guerrero 4, T998-877 0006. Motel-style place with parking. The rooms are good and clean, with fridge, bath and fan. Good value.

$$-$ Posada Edelmar, Hidalgo, next to **Bucanero** hotel and restaurant. Economical alternative slap-bang in the middle of the pedestrianized section of town, seconds from the main restaurants and bars. Spacious rooms with good showers. Ask for a room at the back if you want some peace and quiet.

$$-$ Vistalmar, Av Rueda Medina on promenade close to the ferry dock and Pemex station, T998-877 0209 (**$** for longer stays). Clean, comfortable rooms with fan, bath, balcony and TV. Some have a/c (**$$**). Ask for a room on the top floor.

$ Hostel Posada del Mar, Av Juárez s/n, T998-100 0759. This hostel, features dorms and a couple of private rooms, all with fan, hot water and safety boxes. Continental breakfast included.

$ Pocna Hostel (price per person), top end of Matamoros on the northeast coast, T998-877 0090, www.pocna.com. This is an island institution. Large, busy and warren-like Pocna has a plethora of dorms and rooms. There's internet access, lounge and beach bar, space to sling a hammock, yoga lessons and live music in the evenings. Book in advance – this is one of few hostels on the island, and as such is popular.

Puerto Morelos *p66*

$$$ Rancho Sak-Ol Libertad, next door to **Caribbean Reef Club**, T998-871 0181, www.rancholibertad.com. Thatched *cabañas*; the price includes breakfast, scuba-diving and snorkelling gear for rent.

$$ Posada Amor, Av Javier Rojo Gómez, opposite the beach, T998-871 0033. Very pleasant, well-built *cabañas* with good mosquito nets, the cheaper ones have outdoor communal showers, there is also a good restaurant and prices are reduced considerably out of season.

Playa del Carmen *p66, map p67*
Accommodation in Playa del Carmen is generally expensive and poor value, particularly around the beach and Av 5. The prices given below are for the high season, and can drop by as much as 50% at other times of the year.

$$$$ Tides Riviera Maya, Rivera Maya Playa, Xcalacoco, Fracc 7, T984-877 3000, www.tidesrivieramaya.com. This boutique hotel boasts 30 well-designed villas in a jungle garden, and unpretentious service. The beach here is rocky, but they have built decking out to the sea so you can swim away from the rocks. See Activities and tours, page 92.

$$$$-$$$ Alhambra, Calle 8 Norte, corner with the beach, T984-873 0735, www.alhambra-hotel.net. Nice, airy palatial feel at this hotel with spiritual inclinations. All rooms have balcony or sea view, and general services include yoga instruction, jacuzzi, massage and there is a spa. Quiet and peaceful, despite its setting near beach bars. Family-run, French and English spoken. Recommended.

$$$ Hotel Cielo, Calle 4, between 5 and 10, T984-873 1227, www.hotelcielo.com. Right in the centre of town, rooms have a/c, cable TV, safe and also throw in beach towels and breakfast. The corridors are a bit dark and narrow, but the views from the roof terrace superb. Great tacos at Restaurant Carboncito, attached.

$$$-$$ Casa Tucán, Calle 4 Norte, between Av 10 and 15, T984-873 0283, www.casa tucan.de. German-owned hotel with simple, rustic *cabañas* and rooms. Rambling and labyrinthine, but there's a lovely lush garden, beautifully painted murals, and a deep pool where diving instruction takes place. There's

also a restaurant, internet café and other handy outlets attached.

$$$-$$ Hotel Las Molcas, near ferry pier, T984-873 0070, www.molcas.com.mx. Strange but interesting architecture at this hotel, where some of the Moorish-style corridors seem to recede into infinity. There's a pool and staff are friendly.

$$$-$$ Mom's Hotel, Calle 4 and Av 30, T984-873 0315, www.momshotel.com, about 5 blocks from bus station or beach. Excellent value, friendly, family-run hotel with a pool. There are studios and apartments and good rates for long-term stays. Recommended.

$$ Happy Gecko, Av 10 between 6 and 8, T984-147 0692, happygeckohotel@yahoo. com. Canadian-owned, this hotel has good rooms with kitchen, fan and bath, some with a/c. Laundry service and movies available.

$$ Posada Marinelly, Av Juárez between Calle 10 and 15, T984-873 0140. Centrally located with light, bright, comfortable rooms. More expensive with a/c (**$$$**). Handy for the **ADO** terminal. Friendly, bit basic.

$$-$ Urban Hostel, Av 10 between 4 and 6, T984-803 3378, urbanhostel@gmail.com. Funky backpackers' place with private rooms and dorms. Price includes breakfast. There's DVD, Xbox, internet and Wi-Fi, 2 terraces and kitchen.

$ Hostel Playa, Av 25 with Calle 8, T984-803 3277, www.hostelplaya.com. A clean, professionally run hostel with various dorms, private rooms, kitchen and lounge space. There's a comfortable, friendly atmosphere. Prices per person, not per room.

Camping
Punta Bete, 10 km north, the right-hand of 3 campsites at the end of a 5-km road, on beach. US$3 for tent, also 2 restaurants and *cabañas*.

Cozumel *p68, map p68 and p69*
Hotels are generally expensive and poor value. Expect prices to drop by up to 50% during low season.

$$$ Amaranto, Calle 5 Sur, Av 15-20, T987-564 4262, www.cozumel.net/bb/amaranto. Lovely thatched-roof Mayan-style bungalows and suites, complete with hammocks. Spanish, English and French are spoken by the owners, Elaine and Jorge. There's a pool, and childcare is available on request.

$$$ Flamingo, Calle 6 Norte 81, T954-315 9236, www.hotelflamingo.com. Tasteful, comfortable rooms with a/c, Wi-Fi, balcony and fridge. There's a penthouse on the roof, good for families. Friendly staff.

$$$ Tamarindo, Calle 4 Norte 421, between Av 20 and 25, T987-872 3614, www.cozumel.net/bb/tamarind. Intimate bed and breakfast, also owned by Elaine and Jorge. There's a shared kitchen, hammocks, dive-gear storage and rinse tank, purified drinking water, laundry, and safe-deposit box.

$$ Pepita, Av 15 Sur 120 y Calle 1 Sur, T987-872 0098, www.hotelpepitacozumel. com. Very pleasant rooms around a plant-filled courtyard. Modern fittings, a/c, cable TV, fridge in all rooms. Free coffee in the morning. Recommended.

$$ Posada Edén, Calle 2 Norte 124, T987-872 1166, gustarimo@hotmail.com. Clean, economical rooms with the usual bare necessities, including fan or a/c. There are apartments for long-term rental, 1 month minimum.

$$ Posada Marruang, A R Salas 440, between Av 20 Sur and 25 Sur, T987-872 1678. Very spick and span, large spartan rooms set back from road; barking dog ensures occasional noise and total security.

$$ Posada Zuanayoli, Calle 6 Norte 272 between Av 10 and Av 15 Norte, T987-872 0690. Tall, old and slightly knackered building in a quiet street. Clean rooms have TV, fridge, fan, some with a/c. Free coffee and drinking water for guests.

$$-$ Flores, A R Salas 72, off plaza, T987-872 1429. A range of basic, acceptable rooms with cable TV, fan or a/c. Only 50 m from the sea and very cheap for the location.

Tulum *p72*
Tulum village

Tulum village is a blossoming, but still relatively uninspiring destination. Scores of new budget hotels and restaurants are opening apace, making it a good base for backpackers and cost-conscious travellers. However, expect to offset those lower hotel rates with additional transport costs. There are no buses to the beach, only taxis and infrequent *colectivos*. For places to stay in Sian Ka'an Biosphere Reserve, see page 89.

$$ Hotel Maya, Av Tulum near the bus station (do not let taxis take you to Hotel Maya Tulum, an altogether much more expensive hotel), T984-871 1234. Large hotel with plenty of economical rooms, all with fan and bath. There's a restaurant next door serving home-cooked Mexican fare.

$$-$ Rancho Tranquilo, far south end of town, T984-871 2784, www.ranchotranquilo. com.mx. Friendly backpackers' place with dorms, *cabañas* and large rooms with private bath. There's also a lounge, library, shared kitchen and verdant garden. Friendly and highly recommended.

$ Mayan Hostel Tulum, Carretera Coba–Boca Paila SN, 400 m from El Crucero, T998-112 1282, www.mayanhostel.com. Private rooms in *palapas*, dorms with a/c, breakfast and internet included in price. Bike rentals, book exchange, free short-term luggage storage.

$ Weary Traveller Hostel, 1 block south of **ADO** bus terminal, T984-871 2390, www.wearytravelerhostel.com. Tulum's premier backpackers' hostel has bunk dorms, a book exchange and internet. They run transport to the beach, regular salsa classes and you can even cook your own food on the BBQ. A good place to meet fellow travellers. Breakfast included.

Tulum beach

A plethora of lodgings run the length of the coast from Tulum ruins to the Sian Ka'an Biosphere reserve. Development has been mercifully low-key, with ramshackle *cabañas* existing alongside luxury ecolodges. There is little infrastructure beyond these hotels, and it's best to reach them by taxi; official rates are posted on a sign at the rank in the village. Expect room costs to vary with views and proximity to the sea. Bear in mind this is a long stretch of beach and it's not always plausible to walk from hotel to hotel.

$$$$ Ana y José, 7 km south of ruins, T984-880 5629, www.anayjose.com. Once only a collection of humble *cabañas*, Ana y José now offer elegant suites and luxurious spa accommodation. First-rate service and attention.

$$$$-$$$ Nueva Vida de Ramiro, Carretera Tulum–Boca Paila Km 8.5, No 17, T984-877 8512, www.tulumnv.com. If you must stay in high-end style in Tulum, these ecobungalows will do the trick. Straight on the beach.

$$$$-$$$ Posada Margherita, T984-801 8493, www.posadamargherita.com. A decent, hospitable hotel with complete wheelchair access. There's 24-hr electricity and an excellent Italian restaurant attached. Recommended.

$$$ Cabañas Diamante K, on the beach quite near the ruins, T984-876 2115, www.diamantek.com. Rustic and friendly, with an array of interesting statues and hints of The Crystal Maze. *Cabaña* prices vary according to location and amenities, much cheaper with shared bath. There's a good bar and restaurant.

$$$ Hotel Zazil-Kin, near the ruins, T984-124 0082, www.zazilkintulum.com. A popular, well-established Tulum favourite. A bit basic for the price, it offers a wide range of lodgings from rooms to *cabañas*, as well as restaurant, bar and gift shop.

$$$-$$ Dos Ceibas, 9 km from the ruins, T984-877 6024, www.dosceibas.com. This verdant ecolodge on the edge of the Sian Ka'an Biosphere reserve has a handful of comfortable *cabañas*. Massage and yoga instruction available. Friendly and tranquil ambience.

$$$-$$ Los Arrecifes, 7 km from ruins, T984-155 2957, www.losarrecifestulum. com. *Cabañas*, trampoline, live music and shows, restaurant.

$$ Playa Condesa, next door to **Diamante K**. Simple, airy wooden *cabañas*, not particularly good value for the price. Electricity a few hours each evening. There's a basic, but pricey grocery shop attached.

$$-$ Mar Caribe, near the ruins. Smaller complex than its neighbour, **Zazil-Kin**, but a friendly atmosphere, and much more peaceful. Very cheap if you bring your own hammock or tent. Organizes tours.

Cobá p74

$$$-$$ Villas Arqueológicas (Club Méditerranée), about 2 km from site on lake shore, T985-858 1527, www.villas arqueologicas.com.mx. Open to non-members, excellent, clean and quiet, a/c, swimming pool, good restaurant with moderate prices, but expensive beer. Don't arrive without a reservation, especially at weekends; and yet making a reservation by phone seems to be practically impossible.

$ Hotel Restaurant El Bocadito, in the village, on the street leading to the main road, T984-876 3738, www.cancunsouth. com/bocadito/. Run-down, spartan rooms with fan, intermittent water supply, poor security, good but expensive restaurant (which is popular with tour groups), books and handicrafts for sale. Recommended.

Sian Ka'an Biosphere Reserve p75

$$$$-$$$ Rancho Sol Caribe, Punta Allen, T984-139 3839, www.solcaribe-mexico.com. 4 comfortable *cabañas*, with bath, restaurant. Very expensive but recommended.

$$$ Centro Ecológico Sian Ka'an, T984-871 2499, www.cesiak.org. Environmentally considerate and sensitive accommodation in the heart of the Reserve. Tours, kayaking and fly fishing arranged.

Felipe Carrillo Puerto *p76*
$$ El Faisán y El Venado, Av Benito Juárez, Lote 781, 2 blocks northeast of main square. Mixed reports on cleanliness, but hot water and good-value restaurant, popular with locals.
$$ María Isabel, near the plaza. Clean, friendly, laundry service, quiet, safe parking.
$$ San Ignacio, Av Benito Juárez 761, near Pemex. Good value, a/c, bath, towels, TV, secure car park.
$$-$ Chan Santa Cruz, Calle 68, 782, just off the plaza, T983-834 0021, www.hotelchansantacruz.com. Good, clean and friendly. A/c, cable TV, handicap accessible, fridge (**Restaurante 24 Horas** is open, as you'd imagine, 24 hrs).

Mahahual and around *p76*
There are plenty of options for sleeping with hammocks, camping and *cabañas*.
$$ Sol y Mar restaurant, en route to Puerto Bravo, near Mahahual, with rooms to rent, bathrooms and spaces for RVs, also coconut palms and beach.
$$-$ Kabah-na, T983-838 8861, www.kabahna.com. *Cabañas* for 2 or space to hang a hammock, right on the beach.
$ Kok Hal, Mahahual, on the beach close to the old wharf. Shared bath and hot showers.

Camping
Camidas Trailer Park, Punta Herrero road, with palm trees, *palapas*, restaurant and space for 4 RVs, US$5 per person, car free.

Chetumal *p77, map p77*
$$$ Los Cocos, Av Héroes de Chapultepec 134, T983-835 0430, www.hotelloscocos. com.mx. Large, professionally managed hotel with clean, comfortable rooms and

suites. There's a pool, bar and restaurant. Recommended.
$$$-$$ Caribe Princess, Av Obregón 168, T983-832 0520, www.caribeprincess chetumal.com. Good, clean rooms with a/c and TV. Recommended.
$$ El Dorado, Av 5 de Mayo 42, T983-832 0315. Comfortable rooms with hot water and a/c. Friendly and quiet. Recommended.
$$ Palma Real, Obregón 103, T983-833 0963. Friendly and helpful place with big, clean rooms. Bath, cable TV and a/c.
$$ Ucúm, Gandhi 167 corner of 16 de Septiembre, T983-832 6186, www.hotel ucumchetumal.com. Rooms with a/c, fan and bath. Pool and enclosed car park. Good-value restaurant next door.
$$-$ Hotel Cristal, Cristóbal Colón 207, T983-832 3878. Simple rooms with fan and bath. Parking available.
$$-$ Real Azteca, Av Belice 186, T983-832 0720. Cheerful, friendly, but no hot shower. 2nd-floor rooms best, but still not too good.
$ María Dolores, Av Alvaro Obregón 206, T983-832 0508. Bath, hot water, fan, clean, windows don't open, noisy, restaurant **Solsimar** downstairs good and popular. Recommended.

Towards Bacalar *p78*
$$$$ Akal Ki, Carretera Federal 307, Km 12.5, Bacalar Lagoon, T983-106 1751, www.akalki.com. A marvellously peaceful retreat with *palapas* built right over the water. Though surrounded by jungle, this strip of the lagoon has few rocks and little vegetation, making it crystal clear and ideal for swimming. Minimum stay 3 days. See Activities and tours, page 93.
$$$ Rancho Encantado, 3 km north of Bacalar, on the west shore of the lagoon. Resort hotel, half-board available, Apdo 233, Chetumal, T983-101 3358, www.encantado. com. With private dock, tour boat, canoes and windsurf boards for rent, private cabins with fridge and hammock, very good. See Activities and tours, page 93.

$$$-$$ Hotel Las Lagunas, Bvl Costero 479, about 2 km south of Bacalar (on left-hand side of the road going towards the village), T983-834 2206. It is very good, wonderful views, helpful, clean, comfortable, hot water, swimming pool and opposite a freshwater lake; restaurant is poor and overpriced.

$$ Hotel América, Av 5 258, Bacalar, 700 m north of the bus stop on the plaza (walk in the opposite direction to Chetumal). Recommended.

Camping

Camping is possible at the end of the road 100 m from the lagoon, toilets and shower, US$0.10, but lagoon perfect for washing and swimming.

Eating

Cancún *p61, maps p62 and p64*
The **Hotel Zone** is lined with expensive restaurants, with every type of international cuisine imaginable, but with a predominance of Tex-Mex and Italian. Restaurants in the centre are cheaper, and the emphasis is on local food.

The cheapest area for dinner is **SM64**, opposite **Plaza 2000**. Popular with locals, especially on Sun when it is hard to get a table; there are 4 or 5 small, family-run restaurants serving local specialities. *Comida corrida* for as little as US$2. **Mercado 28** is the best budget option for breakfast or lunch, with many cheap outdoor and indoor *loncherías* serving *comida corrida*, very popular with locals, quick service. Another good option is **Mercado 23**, 5 blocks north of the ADO terminal, along Calle Cedro.

$$$ El Pescador, Tulipanes 28. Good seafood, well established with excellent reputation. Expensive.

$$$ La Habichuela, Margaritas 25. Award-winning restaurant serving delicious Caribbean seafood in a tropical garden setting. Great ambience and jazz music.

$$$ La Parilla, Yaxchilán 51. Mouth-watering grill platters, ribs and steaks. A buzzing, lively joint, always busy and popular. Try the enormous margaritas in exotic flavours – hibiscus flower and tamarind.

$$$ Pericos, Av Yaxchilán 71, T998-884 3152, www.pericos.com.mx. Chicken, meat, fish fillets and seafood platters at this themed Mexican restaurant where the staff wear fancy dress. It's touristy, it's cheesy, but the atmosphere is great.

$$$-$$ El Rincón del Vino, Alcatraces 29. Tapas with a seafood emphasis. As the name suggests, there's a healthy stock of wine. A tranquil and pleasant place, with a range of international food.

$$$-$$ Labná, Margaritas 29. The best in Yucatecan cooking, serving dishes like *poc chuc* and *pollo pibil*. Try the platter and sample a wide range of this fascinating regional cuisine. Good lunchtime buffet.

$$ El Poblano, Tulum and Tulipanes. Tacos, kebabs, grilled meats and steaks – carnivores call it dinner. A friendly, unpretentious restaurant, popular with Mexicans.

$$ Rincón Yucateco, Av Uxmal 24. Good grills and traditional Mexican grub from lunchtime.

Cafés

Pastelería Italiana, Yaxchilán, just before Sunyaxchén turning. Excellent coffee and pastries, friendly. There are a few other cheap eateries along Yaxchilán, tucked away between the pricey themed restaurants, some open during the day only.

Isla Mujeres *p64*
Hidalgo is the most popular for restaurants.

$$$ Mesón del Bucanero, Hidalgo, opposite **Rolandis**. Steaks, seafood, pasta and crêpes at this classy restaurant. There's a rich offering of cocktails too. Nice al fresco seating.

$$ Bamboo, Hidalgo. A sleek and trendy restaurant-bar serving sushi, Thai curries, seafood and fresh fruit juices. Live music at the weekends.

$$ Comono, Hidalgo. Open 1400-2230, Mon-Fri. Israeli-run kitchen and bar that serves Mediterranean food, beer and shakes. There are nightly movies, live music on Fri, and hookah pipes if you fancy smoking some molasses. Popular with backpackers.

$$ Los Amigos Restaurant, Hidalgo. Small, with 2 tables outside, excellent pizzas and pasta.

$$ Mamma Rosa, Hidalgo and Matamoros. Formerly La Malquerida. Italian-run restaurant serving pasta and seafood with a good selection of Italian wines.

$$ Miguel's Moon Lite, Hidalgo 9. Good hospitality at this lively restaurant-bar. When the booze isn't flowing, there's tacos, steaks and seafood. Ask for a free shot of pomegranate tequila.

$$ Rolandis, Hidalgo, T998-877 0700. Terrace overlooking the street. Excellent Italian food, including a good range of tasty pizzas and pastas, seafood and meat dishes. Has many branches across Mexico.

$ La Susanita, Juárez 5. Excellent home cooking, at this cute little locals' place; when closed it is the family's living room.

$ Lonchería La Lomita, Juárez 25B. Nice and clean and at US$3, quite possibly the best value, tasty food in town.

$ Loncherías, northwest end of Guerrero, around the municipal market. Open till 1800. Busy and bustling, good for breakfast, snacks and lunch. All serve the same local fare at similar prices.

$ Poc-Chuc, Juárez y Madero. Somewhat rough and ready locals' joint, serving up big portions and good *tortas*.

Cafés

Aluxes Café, Av Matamoros, next to **Aquí Estoy Pizza**. A cheery place serving cappuccinos, filter coffee and home-made snacks.

Cafecito, Matamoros 42. Cool and tranquil. A nice breakfast place, serving waffles, juice, sandwiches.

Puerto Morelos *p66*
$$ Johnny Cairo. Good typical food.
$$ Pelícano. Very good seafood.

Playa del Carmen *p66, map p67*
The majority of the town's restaurants line Av 5, where most tourists limit themselves and a meal costs no less (and usually a bit more) than US$10. Popular, big name restaurants dominate the southern end of the street. Quieter, subtler settings lie north, beyond Calle 20. For budget eating, head west, away from the main drag.

$$$ Buenos Aires, Calle 6 Norte between Av 5 and 10, on Plaza Playa. Speciality Argentine meats, run by Argentines, nice for a change from Mexican food.

$$$ The Glass Bar, Calle 10, between Av 1 and 5, www.theglassbar.com.mx. A sophisticated Italian restaurant serving fine wine, Mediterranean cuisine and seafood. The place for an intimate, romantic dinner.

$$$ Karen's, Av 5, between Calle 2 and 4. Always a lively, family atmosphere here. The menu includes Mexican staples, good pizzas, grilled meats and tacos. There's live music most nights. Popular.

$$$ La Parrilla, Av 5 y Calle 8. Large portions, good service, live mariachi band every night, popular.

$$$ Yaxche, Calle 8 between Av 5 and 10. Traditional Maya cuisine. Cheaper lunchtime menu (**$$**).

$$$-$$ Los Comales, Av 5 and Calle 4. Popular seafood restaurant. Dishes include Veracruz fish fillet, seafood platters, surf n turf, *fajitas* and other Mexican fare. There's a good-value breakfast buffet for US$5.50.

$$$-$$ Maktub, Av 5, between Calle 28 and 30. Arab and Lebanese cuisine, clean and pleasant, with outdoor seating.

$$$-$$ Sushi-Tlan, Av 5, between Calle 28 and 30. Something different; a clean, fresh, brightly lit sushi bar.

$$ Pez Vela, Av 5 y Calle 2. Good atmosphere, food, drinks and music.

$$ Rolandi, Av 5, close to the ferry dock. Superb pasta and pizza at this popular Italian place. Branches across Mexico.

$ Billy the Kid, Av 15 and Calle 4. This very cheap, rough-and-ready locals' haunt does tacos and *tortas*.

$ El Fogón, Av 30 and Calle 6. Locals' taco joint that serves grilled meat, wholesome *tortas* and *quesadillas*.

$ Tortas del Carmen, Av 15, between Calle 4 and 2. Tasty *tortas* and *licuados*, open from 0830.

Cafés and bakeries
Java Joe's, Calle 10, between Av 5 and 10. Italian and gourmet coffees, sandwiches, pastries. Next door's café/bookshop **Habita** is worth a peak for its art, books and alternative cultural space.

Cozumel *p68, map p68 and p69*
There are few eating options for budget travellers. The cheapest places for breakfast, lunch or an early dinner are the *loncherías* next to the market on A R Salas, between Av 20 and 25. They serve fairly good local *comida corrida*, 0800-1930.

$$$ Lobster's Cove, Av Rafael Melgar 790, T987-872 4022. Quality seafood, live music, happy hour 1200-1400.

$$$ Pancho's Backyard, Rafael Melgar 27, in **Los Cinco Soles** shopping complex in big courtyard out the back. Mexican food and wine elegantly served, good food.

$$$ Prima, Salas 109. Open 1600-2400. Northern Italian seafood, handmade pasta, brick-oven pizzas, non-smoking area.

$$$-$$ Casa Mission, Av 55, between Juárez and Calle 1 Sur, www.missioncoz.com. Open daily 1700-2300. Established in 1973, this restaurant survived hurricanes Wilma and Gilbert and is now a Cozumel institution. Fine Mexican, international and seafood in an elegant hacienda setting.

$$$-$$ La Choza, Salas 198 and Av 10, www.lachozarestaurant.com. Decent Mexican and regional cuisine. Popular.

$$ Las Palmeras, at the pier (good people-watching spot), Av Melgar. Open 0700-1400. Very popular for breakfast, always busy. Recommended.

$$-$ Casa Deni's, Calle 1 Sur 164, close to plaza. Open-air restaurant, very good, cheapish prices.

Tulum *p72*
Tulum village
Testament to Tulum's growing popularity, a plethora of new restaurants have opened in town, mostly along Av Tulum. Wander along in the evening and take your pick of everything from Argentine *parrillas* to seafood and pizzas.

$$$-$$ El Pequeño Buenos Aires, Av Tulum, Argentine steak and grill house, one great meat feast, open air setting on the main drag.

$$ Don Cafeto, Av Tulum 64. Popular place serving Mexican fare. Usually buzzing in the evenings. Beach branch currently shut, but set to re-open in late 2009.

$$ La Nave, Av Tulum. Italian restaurant and pizzeria, set on 2 floors, nice rustic wooden decor. Cosy in the evenings.

$ Doña Tinas, good basic and cheap, in a grass hut at southern end of town. **El Mariachito** next door also does good, cheap and cheerful grub.

$ El Mariachi, cheap taco bar with good *fajitas*.

Tulum beach
Restaurants on the beach tend to be owned by hotels. For dinner, book in advance where possible. Strolling between establishments after dark isn't advisable.

$$$-$$ La Zebra, Carretera Tulum–Boca Paila Km 7.5, www.lazebratulum.com. Fresh, tasty barbequed fish, shrimps, *ceviche* and Mexican fare. Lashings of Margarita at the **Tequila Bar**.

\$\$\$-\$\$ Mezzanine, Carretera Tulum–
Boca Paila Km 1.5. Excellent authentic
Thai cuisine and Martini bar attached.
\$\$\$-\$\$ Restaurant Margherita,
Carretera Tulum–Boca Paila Km 4.5, in
Posada Margherita. Closed Sun. Excellent,
freshly prepared Italian food in an intimate
setting. Hospitable, attentive service.
Book in advance. Recommended.

Cobá *p74*

There are plenty of restaurants in the village,
on the road to **Villas Arqueológicas** and
on the road to the ruins, all quite pricey.
There's also a grocery store by **El Bocadito**
and souvenir shops.
\$\$ Pirámides, on corner of track leading to
Villas Arqueológicas. Highly recommended.
\$ Nicte-Ha, good and friendly.

Sian Ka'an Biosphere Reserve *p75*

\$\$-\$ La Cantina, Punta Allen, a good,
non-touristy restaurant (US\$3-4 for fish).

Felipe Carrillo Puerto *p76*

\$\$ Danburger Maya, next door to hotel **San
Ignacio**. Good food, reasonable prices, helpful.
\$ Restaurant Addy, on main road, south
of town. Good, simple.

Chetumal *p77, map p77*

\$\$\$-\$\$ El Emporio, Merino 106. Delicious
Uruguayan steaks served in a historic
old house near the bay.
\$\$ Barracuda, about 4 blocks north of
market, then 3 blocks west (another area
with many restaurants). Good seafood.
\$\$ Sergio Pizza, Av Obregón 182. Pizzas,
fish, and expensive steak meals, a/c, good
drinks, excellent service.
\$\$-\$ El Fenicio, Héroes and Zaragoza, open
24 hrs, with mini-market at the back. Chicken,
steaks, burgers and Mexican grub.
\$ Los Milagros, Zaragoza and 5 de Mayo.
This locals' café serves economical Mexican
fare, *comida corrida* and breakfasts.

\$ Mercado. Cheap meals in the market at the
top of Av Héroes, but the service is not too
good and tourists are likely to be stared at.
\$ Pantoja, Ghandi 87. Busy locals' joint
serving the usual economical fare.

Towards Bacalar *p78*
\$\$ La Esperanza, 1 block north from
plaza. Thatched barn, good seafood.
\$\$ Punta y Coma, Orizaba, 3 blocks from
zócalo. Inexpensive, large menu including
vegetarian. Recommended.

⊙ Entertainment

Cancún *p61, maps p62 and p64*
Bars and clubs
The action happens in the Zona Hotelera,
around 9 km from downtown on Kukulcan
Blv, where big clubs play to big crowds.
Girls will often drink for free, and there's a
distinctly North American flavour. Downtown
has a thriving scene too, mostly focused
on Yaxchilán and the surrounding streets.
If you get the chance to see local dance
band **Balancê** (www.balancelabanda.com),
don't miss it.
Bulldog, Blv Kukulcán Km 9, www.bulldog
cafe.com/cancun.html. Rock, hip-hop, pop
and salsa. A popular, well-organized mega
club with sophisticated light and sound rigs.
Coco Bongo, Forum by the Sea mall,
www.cocobongo.com.mx. Open Wed-Sat.
Cancún's most famous nightclub. Expect
wild theatrical displays, including dance,
acrobatics, laser shows and gallons of dry
ice. Loud, pumping dance music is played.
Dady Rock, Blv Kukulcán Km 9.5, www.dady
rock.com.mx. 2 floors, 4 bars, DJs, MCs and
live bands. **Dady Rock** lays on the entertainment with boundless paternal generosity.
There's frequent bikini, 'sexy legs' and 'wet
body' contests too, if that's your sort of thing.
Señor Frog's, Blv Kukulcán Km 9.5,
www.senorfrogs.com. You'll get a yard
glass on entry, fill it with the booze of your
choice, open wide and drink. A notorious

'Spring Break' dive, Señor Frogs is a long-standing Cancún favourite; it's spawned branches in most Mexican resorts and across the Caribbean with an array of dubious, themed merchandise to match. Cover US$5.

Cinemas
Cinepolis, Tulum 260, SM7. Large complex showing English-language, subtitled films.

Isla Mujeres *p64*
Bar and clubs
Most of the bars have a permanent happy hour, with 2 drinks for the price of 1. Happy Hour here also tends to favour women, who sometimes get to drink for free. There are many bars along Hidalgo and the beach – take your pick.
Chile Locos, along the beach, with live marimba music.
La Adelita, Hidalgo 12. Adelita stocks over 200 types of tequila, the bar staff really know their stuff and are happy to make recommendations. Pull up a stool, roll up your sleeves – it's going to be a long night.
La Palapa, on Playa Los Cocos. Serves cocktails and snacks and is busy during the day until everyone leaves the beach, then fills up again after midnight for drinking and dancing.
Om Bar, Matamoros 15. Open Wed-Sat, from 1900. Chilled-out hippy lounge. Drink beer and cocktails under the *palapa*, relax to reggae or Latin jazz. Free shots.

Playa del Carmen *p66, map p67*
Bars and clubs
Nightlife in Playa del Carmen is famously hedonistic. The best clubs are situated on Calle 12 and 14. There are also some bars in the 'gringo zone' by the ferry dock – **Señor Frog's** and **Carlos 'n' Charlies**, most notably.
Beer Bucket, Calle 10, between Av 5 and 10. Want a simple, unpretentious beer? Try this place, popular with expats, where the grog and conversation flow cheaply.

Blue Parrot Inn, Calle 12 y Av 1, next to beach. Dance, trance and house at this famous, sexy nightclub on the beach. Ladies night on Mon and Thu, with free drinks.
Coco Maya, Calle 12 and the beach. Beach club playing R and B, hip-hop, house and dance. Lots of TV screens, all under a *palapa*.
El Cielo, Calle 12, between Av 5 and the beach. Swanky disco playing dance and pumping tunes. Popular and well-known. Cover for men US$5, women free.
Habibi and Los Aguachiles, next door to OM (below) are upmarket and trendy watering holes for the hip and happening. Worth a peek, if a bit pricey.
OM, Calle 12, between Av 5 and the beach. Suave lounge-bar with sofas, sheeshas and ethereal white drapes. Electronic music.
Tequila Barrel, Av 5 between Calle 10 and 12. Tex-Mex Bar and grill, friendly owner (Greco) and staff. Girls who dance on the bar get a free shot of tequila.

Cozumel *p68, map p68 and p69*
Bars and clubs
1.5 Tequila Lounge, Melgar and Calle 11 Sur. Boozy, sociable lunch bar, popular with visitors straight off the cruise ships.
Carlos 'n Charlies, Plaza Punta Langosta. Big-name chain bar, always busy with tourists.
Neptuno, Melgar and Calle 11 Sur. Long-standing Cozumel disco, playing salsa, dance and reggae.
Señor Frog's, Plaza Punta Langosta, www.senorfrogs.com. Chain bar popular with North Americans and other tourists.

Shopping

Cancún *p61, maps p62 and p64*
There are several US-style shopping malls in the Hotel Zone. The main one, **Plaza Kukulcán**, known as Luxury Avenue, www.luxuryavenue.com, has over 200 shops, restaurants, a bowling alley and video games. It is open daily 1000-2200, and the prices are high for most things, including souvenirs. The

main **craft market** is on Av Tulum near Plaza Las Américas; it is a huge network of stalls, all selling exactly the same merchandise: silver jewellery from Taxco, ceramic Maya figurines, hammocks, jade chess sets. Prices are hiked up to the limit, so bargain hard: most vendors expect to get half what they originally ask for. The market called **Mercado 23** (at the end of Calle Cedro, off Av Tulum) has cheaper souvenirs and less aggressive salesmen it's a bit tatty and tacky, although good for cheap food; *guayabera* shirts are available on one of the stalls. Several smoking shops have appeared, cashing in on the craze for Cuban cigars; (inspect your purchase thoroughly – if the price seems too good to be true, rest assured that it is); these are all located on or just off Av Tulum. Note that genuine Cuban cigars will be seized by US Customs if entering the States. Cheaper clothes shops than the Hotel Zone can be found at the north end of Av Tulum, near Plaza 2000. Pricey leather goods, clothes and jewellery can be bought in the **Plaza 2000** shopping mall.

Isla Mujeres *p64*
Cigars
Tobacco & Co, Hidalgo 14. Cuban cigars and smoking paraphernalia. There are several other shops in the centre selling Cuban cigars.

Souvenirs
Av Hidalgo is lined with souvenir shops, most of them selling the same things: ceramic Maya figurines and masks; hammocks; blankets; and silver jewellery from Taxco. Bargaining is obligatory – try and get the desired item for half the original asking price, which is what the vendors expect to receive. There are more souvenir shops along the harbour front, where the salesmen are more pushy, and more shops along **Av Morelos**.

Playa del Carmen *p66, map p67*
Lots of expensive souvenir shops clustered around the plaza; cheaper shops, for day-to-day items, are on Av Juárez. There's a cheap *panadería* at the beginning of Av Juárez. For developing photos and buying film, there are several places along Av 5.

Chetumal *p77, map p77*
Shops are open 0800-1300, 1800-2000. Av Héroes is the main shopping street. Good for foreign foodstuffs – cheaper at the covered market in the outskirts than in the centre.

▲ Activities and tours

Cancún *p61, maps p62 and p64*
Boat trips and cruises
Aquaworld, Blv Kukulcán 15.2, T998-848 8327, www.aquaworld.com.mx. A range of boat trips and cruises including day-trips to Isla Mujeres and Cozumel; dinner cruises on the 'Cancun Queen'; and underwater explorations on their 'Sub See Explorer' submarine. They also organize parasailing, jungle tours and swimming with dolphins.

Bullfighting
Plaza de Toros, Av Bonompak south, has a folkloric show and bullfight every Wed at 1530, 2½ hrs. Admission US$38, tickets available at travel agents and the ring.

Dolphin encounters
Dolphin Discovery, Kukulcán Km 5, T998-849 4748, www.dolphindiscovery.com. Splash around with dolphins, manatees and seals, and get in touch with your inner sea mammal. A real winner for families.

Golf
Club de Golf Cancun, Kukulcán Km 7.5, T998-883 1230, www.cancungolfclub.com, 18-hole championship course, driving range and putting greens.
Hilton Cancun Beach and Golf Resort, Kukulcán Blv Km 17, T998-881 8000,

www.hiltoncancun.com/golf.htm.
An attractive 18-hole course on the
banks of a lagoon.

Scuba-diving and snorkelling
See also Aquaworld, above.
Scuba Cancun, Kukulcán Km 5, T998-
849 5226, www.scubacancun.com.mx.
A medium-sized dive centre run by
Captain Luis Hurtado who has 54 years'
diving experience. It offers a range of dives,
snorkelling tours and accelerated PADI courses.

Tour operators
American Express, Av Tulum 208,
esq Agua, SM 4, T998-884 5441.
Mayan Destinations, Cobá 31, Edif
Monaco, SM22, T998-884 4308, www.mayan
destinations.com. All the usual destinations,
such as Chichén Itzá, Xcaret, Tulum, as well
as flights to Cuba. Many others in the centre
and at larger hotels. Most hotels on the hotel
zone have their own travel agency.

Water sports
A variety of watersports can be organized
on the beaches along the hotel zone,
including parasailing, waterskiing,
windsurfing and jet-skiing.

Isla Mujeres *p64*
Birdwatching
Amigos de Isla Contoy, T998-884 7483,
www.amigosdeislacontoy.org and
www.islacontoy.org. This environmental
organization keeps lists of authorized tour
boats to Isla Contoy – a protected bird
sanctuary, 30 km north of Isla Mujeres.
More than 10,000 birds spend the winter
on this island, including cormorants,
frigates, herons, boobies and pelicans.

Scuba-diving and snorkelling
Carey, Av Matamoros 13-A, T998-877 0763.
Small groups, bilingual staff and good range

of dives, including reef dives, night dives,
cenote dives and whale shark swimming.
El Garrafón, southern tip of the island,
T998-193 3360, www.garrafon. com. This
watersports centre offers a range of diving
and snorkelling programmes, with a sunken
cross off-shore for divers to explore. They also
do dolphin encounters, kayaking and cycling.
Sea Hawk, Zazil-Ha (behind **Hotel Na-
Balam**) T998-877 1233, seahawkdivers@
hotmail.com. Certified PADI instructors,
2-tank dive US$50, introductory course
including shallow dive US$85. Also
snorkelling trips and fishing trips.

Tour operators
Mundaca Travel, Av Rueda Medina,
T998-877 0845, inside the ferry terminal.
Tours to Chichén Itzá, Tulum, Xel-Ha and
Xcaret. Bus tickets and flights to Cuba.
Friendly and helpful.

Playa del Carmen *p66, map p67*
Massage
Tides Riviera Maya, see Sleeping, page 82.
Offers yoga, *temazcal*, massage, a range of
other therapies, jacuzzis and steam rooms.

Scuba-diving and snorkelling
Abyss, Av 1a, between Calle 10 and 12,
T984-873 2164, www.abyssdiveshop.com,
inside **Hotel Tropical Casablanca**. Said to
be the best. Run by fully certified Canadian
Instructor David Tomlinson. Services include
PADI courses; reef, night and *cenote* dives.
Good value dive packages.
Tank-Ha, Calle 10, between Av 5 and 10,
T984-873 0302, www.tankha.com.
Experienced and well-established dive
centre offering a range of packages.
Yucatek Divers, Av 15 Norte, between
Calle 2 and 4, T984-803 2836, www.yucatek-
divers.com. Open 0730-1730. General diving
and snorkelling, including programmes for
disabled people. Also a snorkelling with
whale sharks option.

Tour operators
Alltournative, Av 5, between Calle 12 and 14 and another office between Calle 2 and 4 (opposite the **ADO** terminal), T984-803 9999, www.alltournative.com. Open daily 0900-1900. Culturally and ecologically sensitive tours have won this company several awards. Services include tours to archaeological sites, Mayan villages, forests, lagoons and *cenotes*.
Viajes Felgueres, Calle 6 between Av 5 and Av 10, T984-873 0142. Long-standing and reliable agency with a branch in Cancún, tours to Chichén Itzá, including transport from hotel, guide, entry, food, also bookings for national and international flights, helpful staff.

Cozumel *p68, map p68 and p69*
Scuba-diving
See box, Cenote diving, page 76. The island is famous for the beauty of its underwater environment. The best reef for scuba-diving is **Palancar**, reached only by boat. Also highly recommended are **Santa Rosa** and **Colombia**. For more experienced divers the reefs at **Punta Sur**, **Maracaibo** and **Baracuda** should not to be missed. There are at least 20 major dive sites. Almost all Cozumel diving is drift diving, so if you are not used to a current, choose an operator you feel comfortable with.

Dive centres There are 2 different types of dive centre: the larger ones, where the divers are taken out to sea in big boats with many passengers; the smaller, more personalized dive shops, with a maximum of 8 people per small boat.

The best of the smaller centres is said to be **Deep Blue**, A R Salas 200, corner of Av 10 Sur, T987-872 5653, www.deepblue cozumel.com. Matt and Deborah, an English/Colombian couple, run the centre. All PADI and NAUI certifications, eg 3- to 5-day dive packages US$207-325; cavern and *cenote* diving, including 2 dives, transport and lunch.

Other small dive centres are: **Black Shark**, Av 5 between A R Salas and Calle 3 Sur, T987-872 5657, www.blackshark.com.mx;

Blue Bubble Divers, Carretera Costera Sur Km 3.5, T987-872 4240, www.blue bubble.com; **Diving Adventures**, Calle 15 Sur, between Av 19 and 21, T987-872 3009, www.divingadventures.net.

Decompression centres Buceo Médico Mexicano, Calle 5 Sur No 21B, T987-872 1430, immediate localization (24-hr) VHF 16 and 21. It is supported by US$1 per day donations from divers with affiliated operators. **Cozumel Hyperbarics** in Clínica San Miguel, Calle 6 Norte No 135 between Av 5 and Av 10, T987-872 3070, VHF channel 65.

Tulum *p72*
Diving
Several dive shops all along the Tulum corridor. See box, page 76, for cave diving operators and specialist courses – highly recommended if you like diving. There are many untrained snorkelling and diving outfits, so take care.

Massage
Eco Tulum, www.ecotulum.com. Offers affordable local Maya treatments including clay massage. Yoga, *temazcal* and holistic massage also available.

Chetumal *p77, map p77*
Tour operators
Bacalar Tours, Alvaro Obregón 167A, T987-832 3875, Tours to Mayan ruins and car rental.
Tu-Maya, Alvaro Obregón 312, T983-832 0555, www.casablancachetumal.com/tumaya. 1-day tours to Guatemala, Belize and Calakmul.

Towards Bacalar *p78*
Massage
Akal Ki (see page 85), www.akalki.com. A retreat offering yoga, meditation, *temazcal* and *jenzu*, a seawater massage.
Rancho Encantado (see Sleeping, page 85), www.encantado.com. A holistic resort

offering *lomi lomi*, a form of massage, *temazcal*, *qigong* and meditation.

🔄 Transport

Cancún *p61, maps p62 and p64*
Air
Cancún airport (CUN) has expensive shops and restaurant, exchange facilities, double check your money, especially at busy times, poor rates too, 2 hotel reservation agencies (no rooms under US$45). 2 terminals: **Main** and **South** (or 'FBO' building), white shuttle minibuses between them. From Cancún there are domestic flights and connections throughout the country. For international connections, see Getting there on page 8.

Airline offices Aviacsa, Aerocosta, Tulum 29, T998-884 0383; **Aeromar**, airport, T998-886 1100; **AeroMéxico**, Cobá 80, T998-287 1868; **Aviasca**, Cobá 39, T01-800-284 2272; **Continental Airlines**, airport, T998-886 0006; **Delta airlines**, airport, T998-886 0668.

Bus
For ferries to Isla Mujeres, several buses to the terminals at Gran Puerto and Puerto Juárez run from Av Tulum – try R-13, or R-1 marked Pto Juárez, US$0.80. Taxi to Puerto Juárez, US$2.50.

Long distance Cancún bus terminal, at the junction of Av Tulum and Uxmal, is small, well organized and handy for the cheaper hostels. The bus station is the hub for routes west to Mérida and south to Tulum and Chetumal, open 24 hrs, left luggage from US$0.30 per small bag, per hr, prices rising depending on size of bag, open 0600-2200. To **Cancun Airport**, every 30 mins, 30 mins, US$3.50. To **Chetumal**, ADO, frequent departures, 6 hrs, US$17.50. To **Chichén Itzá**; all 2nd-class buses to Mérida stop here, fewer 1st-class buses, 4 hrs, US$7.50-11.50. To **Mérida**, ADO, frequent departures, 4½ hrs, US$15. To **Palenque**, 1st class (ADO and OCC), 1415, 1545, 1930, 2030, 12½ hrs, US$40; and an

ADO GL, 1745, 13 hrs, US$48. To **Playa del Carmen** ADO shuttle, every 10 mins, 1 hr, US$3. To **Puerto Morelos**, ADO, frequent departures, 30 mins, US$1. To **San Cristóbal**, OCC, 1415, 1545, 2030 18 hrs, US$49, **ADO GL**, 1745, US$58. To **Tulum**, ADO, frequent departures, 2½ hrs, US$5, and many cheaper 2nd-class buses. To **Valladolid**, frequent departures, 2½ hrs, US$9. To **Villahermosa**, 1st class, many departures, 13 hrs, US$52.50-73.50. To **Xcaret**, frequent departures, 1¾ hrs, US$3. To **Xel-Há**, frequent departures, 2 hrs, US$4. **Expreso de Oriente** also has services to the more obscure destinations of **Tizimín** (3 hrs, US$8), **Izamal**, **Cenotillo** and **Chiquilá**.

Car
Car hire There are many car hire agencies, with offices on Av Tulum, in the Hotel Zone and at the airport; look out for special deals, but check vehicles carefully. They include: **Budget**, Av Tulum 231, T998-884 6955; **Alamo**, Cancún Airport, T998-886 0179; **Payless**, Blv Luid Colosio Km 12, T998-886 2812; **Master Car**, Av Uxmal 20, T01-800-711-3344; **Top Rent a Car**, Blv Kukulcán Km 14.5.

Car parking Do not leave cars parked in side streets; there is a high risk of theft. Use the parking lot on Av Uxmal.

Ferry
Ferries to **Isla Mujeres** depart from terminals at Gran Puerto and nearby Puerto Juárez, north of Av Tulum, every 30 mins between 0600-2300, 20 mins by fast ferry, US$2.50, US$5 return (doesn't need to be on the same day). The car ferry departs from Punta Sam, US$18.50 for a driver and vehicle, US$1.50 for each additional passenger.

Isla Mujeres *p64*
Air
The small airstrip in the middle of the island is mainly used for private planes, best arranged with a tourist office in Cancún.

Bicycle and moped

Many touts along Hidalgo offer moped rentals at similar rates: US$7 per hr, US$25 full day. **Sport Bike**, Av Juárez y Morelos, has good bikes. **Cárdenas**, Av Guerrero 105, T998-877 0079, for mopeds and golf carts. Bicycles are usually offered by the same places as mopeds for about US$11 per day.

Bus

A public bus runs from the ferry dock to Playa Paraíso every 30 mins, US$0.30. Timings can be erratic, especially on Sun.

Ferry

For information on ferries to and from the island, see Cancún, above.

Taxi

A taxi from town to **El Garrafón** and vice versa is US$4.30. For the return journey, sharing a taxi will work out marginally more expensive than the bus for 4 people. A taxi from El Garrafón to the bus stop at Playa Paraíso is US$1. Taxis charge an additional US$1 at night. Beware that the prices are fixed, but inflated on this stretch and a taxi ride to the southernmost tip of the island, a short walk from El Garrafón, is cheaper at US$2.80.

Golf carts There are several places renting golf carts, eg **Ciros**, on Matamoros near Playa Cocos. Rates are generally US$32-39 per day. A credit card is usually required as a deposit.

Puerto Morelos *p66*
Bus

There are buses to **Cancún** and **Playa del Carmen** every 30 mins. Buses depart from the main road, taxi to bus stop US$3.

Ferry

Car ferries to **Cozumel** depart at 0500, 1030, 1600, the dock is 500 m south of the plaza. They return at 0800, 1330, 1900, but always check schedules in advance.

Taxi from Cancún airport to Puerto Morelos costs US$25-35.

Playa del Carmen *p66, map p67*
Air

There are flights to **Cozumel** from the nearby airstrip, speak to a tourist office in Playa del Carmen about chartering a plane.

Bus

The **ADO** bus terminal is on Av Juárez between Av 5 and 10. All buses depart from here. The following prices and times are for ADO buses (1st class, a/c, usually showing a video on longer journeys); **Premier**, also 1st class; **Maya de Oro**, supposed to be 1st class but quality of buses can be poor; **OCC**, good 1st-class service. To **Cancún**, frequent departures, 1½ hrs, US$3; 2nd-class services with **Mayab**, less frequent, US$2. To **Cancún airport**, Riviera, frequent between 0700 and 1915, 1 hr, US$6.50. To **Chetumal**, ADO, frequent departures, 4½ hrs, US$14.50; and many 2nd-class buses. To **Chichén Itzá**, 4 departures, 0610, 0730, 0800, 1150, 4 hrs, US$8.50-15.50. To **Mérida**, frequent departures, 5 hrs, US$20.50. To **Mexico City**, ADO, 1230, 1930, 2130, 24½ hrs, US$87. To **San Cristóbal de las Casas**, OCC, 1545, 1715, 2200, 16 hrs, US$46.50; an ADO GL, 1900, US$55.50; and 3 TRF departures, US$30. To **Tulum**, frequent departures, 1 hr, US$3.50. To **Valladolid**, frequent, 3 hrs, US$8.50 (most buses going to Mérida stop at Valladolid. 2nd-class buses to Valladolid go via Tulum). To **Xcaret**, frequent departures, 15 mins, US$0.80. To **Xel Há**, frequent departures, 1 hr, US$3.50.

Car

Car hire Avis, T984-873 1964; **Budget**, 3s and 5a, T984-873 2772; **Executive**, 5a and 12N, T984-873 2354, **Happy Rent a Car**, 10a and Constituyentes, T984-873 1739; **Hertz Rent-a-Car**, Plaza Marina, T984-873 0703; **Rodar**, 5a between 2 and 4, T984-873 0088.

Ferry

Ferries to **Cozumel** depart from the main dock, just off the plaza. There are 2 competing companies, right next to each other, journeys take 30 mins with both, hourly departures on the hour from 0500 until 2200, US$20 return, more to bring a car across. Buy ticket 1 hr before journey.

Taxi

Cancún airport US$35. Beware of those who charge only US$5 as they are likely to charge an extra US$20 for luggage. Tours to **Tulum** and **Xel-Há** from kiosk by boat dock US$30; tours to Tulum, Xel-Há and **Xcaret**, 5-6 hrs, US$60; taxi to Xcaret US$6.65. Taxis congregate on the Av Juárez side of the square (**Sindicato Lázaro Cárdenas del Río**, T998-873 0032).

Cozumel *p68, map p68 and p69*
Airline offices

Most are based at the airport, 2 km north of the town. **Continental**, T987-872 0847. **Mexicana**, P Joaquín between Salas and Calle 3 Sur, next to Pemex, T987-872 0157.

Bicycle and moped

There is no bus service, but taxis are plentiful. The best way to get around the island is by hired moped or bicycle. Mopeds cost US$25-35 per day, credit card needed as deposit; bicycles are around US$15 per day, US$20 cash or TC deposit. **El Aguila**, Av Melgar, between 3 and 5 Sur, T987-872 0729; and **El Dorado**, Av Juárez, between 5 and 10, T987-872 2383.

Car

Car rental There are many agencies, including **Avis**, airport, T987-872 0219; **Budget**, Av 5 between 2 and 4 Norte, T987-872 0219; **Hertz**, Av Melgar, T987-872 3955; **Ejecutivo**, 1 Sur No 19, T987-872 1308.

Tulum *p72*
Bicycle

Bikes can be hired in the village from **Iguana Bike Shop**, Calle Satélite Sur and **Andrómeda**, T984-119 0836 (mob) or T984-871 2357; a good way to visit local centres (**Cristal** and **Escondido** which are recommended as much cheaper, US$2, and less commercialized than **Xcaret**).

Bus

Regular buses go up and down the coastal road travelling from Cancún to Tulum en route to Chetumal, stopping at most places in between. Some buses may be full when they reach Tulum; very few buses begin their journeys here. To **Chetumal**, frequent departures, 4 hrs, 2nd class, US$10, 1st class US$12. To **Cobá**, 8 departures daily, 45 mins, US$3. To **Escárcega**, ADO, 1645, 1715, 7 hrs, US$24.50. To **Felipe Carrillo Puerto**, frequent departures, 1½ hrs, US$5. To **Mérida**, ADO, 2400, 0140, 0500, 1240, 1430, 4 hrs, US$14; and several 2nd-class departures. To **Mexico City**, ADO, 1340, 23½ hrs, US$85. To **Palenque**, OCC, 1655, 1825, 10-11 hrs, US$34; and **ADO GL**, 2015, US$40.50. To **San Cristóbal**, OCC, 1655, 1825, 15 hrs, US$43.50; and an **ADO GL**, 2015, US$52. To **Villahermosa**, ADO, 1340, 2324, 11 hrs, US$38.

Taxi

Tulum town to Tulum ruins US$3.50. To the *cabañas* US$3.50. To **Cobá** about US$25 1 way – bargain hard. **Tucan Kin** run shuttles to Cancún airport, T01-800-702-4111 for reservations, about US$20-25 for 2 people, 1 hr 45 mins.

Cobá *p74*
Bus

Buses into the village turn round at the road end. To **Cancún**, ADO, 1330, 1530, 3 hrs, US$8. To **Playa del Carmen**, ADO, 1330, 1530, 2 hrs, US$5. To **Tulum**, ADO, 1330, 1530, 1 hr, US$2.50.

Taxi

A taxi to **Tulum** should cost you around US$25. If you miss the bus there is a taxi to be found at El Bocadito.

Felipe Carrillo Puerto *p76*
Bus

Bus station opposite Pemex. To **Cancun**, frequent 1st and 2nd-class departures, 4 hrs, US$13. To **Chetumal**, frequent departures, 2½ hrs, US$8. To **Playa del Carmen**, frequent departures, 2½ hrs, US$9. To **Tulum**, frequent departures, 1½ hrs, US$5.

Chetumal *p77, map p77*
Air

Airport (CTM) 2.5 km from town. Flights to **Cancún**, **Mérida**, **Belize City**, **Mexico City**, **Monterrey** and **Tijuana**.

    Airline offices Aviacsa, T983-832 7765.

Bus

Bus information T983-832 5110. The main bus terminal is 3 km out of town at the intersection of Insurgentes y Belice. Taxi into town US$1.50. There is a bus into the centre from Av Belice. **Left-luggage** lockers cost US$0.20 per hr. If buying tickets in advance, go to the **ADO** office on Av Belice esq Ghandi, 0800-1600. There are often more buses than those marked on the display in the bus station. Always ask at the information desk. Many buses going to the border, US$0.30; taxi from Chetumal to border, 20 mins, US$6 for 2. Long-distance buses are often all booked a day ahead, so avoid unbooked connections. Expect passport checks on buses leaving for Mexican destinations.

    To **Bacalar**, very frequent 1st- and 2nd-class departures, 1 hr, US$2. To **Campeche**, ADO, 1200, 6 hrs, US$20. To **Cancún**, many 1st-class departures, 6 hrs, US$17.50. To **Córdoba**, ADO, 1130, 16 hrs, US$57. To **Emiliano Zapata**, 1st class (OCC and ADO), 2150, 2345, 6½ hrs, US$20.50. To

Escárcega, ADO, 11 daily, 4 hrs, US$13. To **Felipe Carrillo Puerto**, many 1st- and 2nd-class departures, 2½ hrs, US$8. To **Mérida**, ADO, 0730, 1330, 1700, 2330, 5½ hrs, US$21. To **Mexico City**, ADO, 1130, 1630, 20½ hrs, US$73.50. To **Minatitlán**, ADO, 2000, 12 hrs, US$36. To **Palenque**, OCC, 0220, 2020, 2150, 7 hrs, US$23; and ADO GL, 2350, US$27. To **Playa del Carmen**, frequent 1st- and 2nd-class departures, 5 hrs, US$14.50. To **Puebla**, ADO, 2300, 17 hrs, US$66.50. To **San Cristóbal**, OCC, 0220, 2020, 2150, 12 hrs, US$33; and ADO GL 2350, US$39.50. To **Tulum**, frequent 1st- and 2nd-class departures, 4 hrs, US$12. To **Tuxtla Gutiérrez** OCC, 2030, 2150, 13 hrs, US$36.50; and ADO GL 2350, US$43.50. To **Veracruz**, 1830, 17 hrs, US$50. To **Villahermosa**, ADO, 6 daily, 8½ hrs, US$27. To **Xpujil**, 13 ADO, Sur and OCC, 2 hrs, US$6.

    To Belize Premier run buses between Chetumal and **Belize City**, 1145, 1445, 1745, 5 hrs, US$10. En route, they stop at **Orange Walk**, 2½ hrs, US$5. Money-changers in the bus terminal offer marginally poorer rates than those at the border. If intending to stay in Belize City, do not take a bus that arrives at night as you are advised not to look for a hotel in the dark.

    To Guatemala Línea Dorada operate daily buses to **Flores** in Guatemala at 0600, US$29. Schedules are very subject to change, and sometimes-lengthy searches are always a possibility, so always check times in advance, and be prepared to spend a night in Chetumal if necessary.

Car

There's a petrol/gas station just outside Chetumal on the road north at the beginning of the road to Escárcega, and another at Xpujil.

Garage Talleres Barrera, helpful, on Primo de Verdad; turn east off Héroes, then past the electrical plant.

Taxi
There are no city buses; taxis run on fixed-price routes, US$1.50 on average. Cars with light-green licence plates are a form of taxi.

Colectivos To **Bacalar** and **Francisco Villa** (for Kohunlich and Xpujil) depart from the junction of Av Miguel Hidalgo and Francisco Primo de Verdad.

Directory

Cancún *p61, maps p62 and p64*
Banks There are 11 Mexican banks along Av Tulum, all in SM4 and SM5. **American Express**, for changing their own TCs at better rates than anywhere else, is on Av Tulum, just south of Av Cobá. Many *casas de cambio* in the centre, mainly around the bus terminal and along Av Tulum. *Casas de cambio* in the Hotel Zone give slightly lower rates for TCs than those in the centre. **Cultural centres** Casa Tabasco, Av Tulum 230, displays and handicrafts for sale from the state of Tabasco, a good place to go if bored of the same old souvenirs in Cancún. **Embassies and consulates** Austria, Cantera 4, SM15, Centro, T998-884 7505. **Canada**, Plaza Caracol, 3rd floor, Hotel Zone, T998-883 3360. **France**, Fonatur St, T998-267 9722. **Germany**, Punta Conoco 36, SM24, Centro, T998-884 1598; **Italy**, Alcatraces 39, SM22, Centro, T998-884 1261. **Netherlands**, Hotel Presidente, Hotel Zone, T998-883 0200. **Spain**, Oasis Corporativo, Hotel Zone, T998-848 9900. **Sweden**, **Switzerland**, Av Cobá 12, T998-884 8446. **UK**, Hotel Royal Sands, Hotel Zone, T998-881 0100. **USA**, Plaza Caracol, 3rd floor, Hotel Zone, T998-883 0272. **Immigration office** On the corner of Av Náder and Av Uxmal. There is also an office in the airport, T998-886 0492, where the staff are better trained and speak English. **Internet** Numerous cafés charging

US$1-1.50 per hr. Generally good servers, open until around 2300. **Language schools** El Bosque del Caribe, Av Náder 52 and Uxmal, T998-884 1065, www.cancun-language.com.mx. **Laundry** Alborada, Nader 5, behind tourist information building on Av Tulum. **Cox-boh**, Av Tankah 26, SM24. **Medical services** American Hospital (24-hr), Viento 15, Centro, T998-884 6133. **Total Assist** (24-hr) Claveles 5, Centro, T998-884 1058. **American Medical Centre**, Plaza Quetzal, Hotel Zone Km 8, T998-883 0113. **Post** At the end of Av Sunyaxchén, near Mercado 28, Mon-Fri 0800-1900, Sat 0900-1300. **Telephone** Many public phones and call shops everywhere, phone cards available from general stores and pharmacies. Collect calls can be made without a card. Also many public phones designed for international calls, which take coins and credit cards. Fax at post office, Mon-Sat, and at San Francisco de Asís shopping mall, Mon-Sat until 2200.

Isla Mujeres *p64*
Banks HSBC, Av Reuda Medina, opposite the ferry dock. Good rates, varying daily, are offered by several *casas de cambio* on Av Hidalgo. The one opposite **Rolandis** is open daily 0900-2100. **Internet** Several internet cafés operate on the island US$1.50 per hr, but speeds can be a little slow. Many cafés and restaurants have free Wi-Fi. **Laundry** Tim Pho, Juárez y Abasolo. **Medical services** Doctors: Dr Antonio Salas, Hidalgo, next to **Farmacia**, T998-877 0477. 24 hrs, house calls, English spoken, air ambulance. **Post** At the end of Guerrero towards the beach. **Telephone** Phone cards can be bought at some of the souvenir shops along Hidalgo.

Puerto Morelos *p66*
Internet There is an internet café on the corner of the plaza opposite **Posada Amor**, US$2.50 per hr, Mon-Sat 1000-1400, 1600-2100.

Playa del Carmen *p66, map p67*
Banks Bancomer, Av Juárez between Calle 25 and 30. **Banamex**, Av Juárez between Calle 20 and 25. A few doors down is **Santander**. Banorte, Av 5 between Av Juárez and the beach. **Inverlat**, Av 5 between Av Juárez and Calle 2. HSBC, Av Juárez between Calle 10 and 15, also at Av 30 between Calle 4 and 6. There are several *casas de cambio* along Av 5, which change TCs with no commission. Count your money carefully as short changing is not uncommon and rates can be hit and miss. **Immigration office** Centro Comercial, Plaza Antigua, Av 10 Sur, T984-873 1884. **Internet** All the cybercafés in town charge between US$1.50-2 per hr. **Language schools** Playalingua,Calle 20 between Av 5 and 10, T984-873 3876, www.playalingua.com, weekend excursions, a/c, library, family stays, US$85 enrolment fee, US$220 per wk (20 hrs). **Solexico Language and Cultural Center**, Av 35 between 6 and 6 bis, T984-873 0755, www.solexico.com. Variable programme with workshops, also have schools in Oaxaca and Puerto Vallarta. **Laundry** Av Juárez, 2 blocks from bus station; another on Av 5. **Maya Laundry**, Av 5 between Calle 2 and Calle 4, Mon-Sat 0800-2100. Laundry in by 1000, ready in the afternoon, many others around town. **Medical services** Dentist: Perla de Rocha Torres, Av 20 Norte between 4 and 6, T984-873 0021, speaks English. Recommended. **International Medical Services: Dr Victor Macías Orosco**, Av 35 between Calle 2 and 4, T984-873 0493. 24-hr emergency service, land and air ambulance, ultrasound, most major insurance accepted. **Tourist Divers Medical Centre**, Dr Mario Abarca, Av 10 between Av Juárez and Calle 2, T984-873 0512. Air and land ambulance service, hyperbaric and diving medicine, affiliated with South Miami Hospital, all insurance accepted. **Police** Av Juárez, T984-873 0291. **Post** Calle 2 and Av 20, Mon-Fri 0800-1700, Sat 0900-1300.

Cozumel *p68, map p68 and p69*
Banks 4 banks on the main square (all with ATMs), all exchange money in morning only, but not at same hours: HSBC, on Juárez, Bancomer, Banamex, Banorte. *Casas de cambio* on Av 5 Norte and around square.
Internet Several internet cafés charging around US$1.50 per hr. **Laundry** Express, Salas between Av 5 and Av 10, T987-872 3655. Coin-op, service washes, US$9 medium load, collection service and dry cleaning.
Medical services Dentist: Dr Hernández, T987-872 0656. Hospitals and clinics: Red Cross, A R Salas between Calle 20 and 25 Sur, T987-872 1058. **Centro Médico de Cozumel**, Calle 1 Sur No 101, esq Av 50, T987-872 3545. English spoken, international air ambulance, 24-hr emergency service. **Pharmacy**: Salas between Av 12 and Av 20, 0700-2400.
Post Av Rafael Melgar y Calle 7 Sur, Mon-Fri 0900-1800, Sat 0900-1200. **Telephone** Ladatel phones (if working) on main square at corner of Av Juárez and Av 5, or on Salas, just up from Av 5 Sur, opposite **Roberto's Black Coral Studio.** For calls to the US, go to **The Stadium**. Telmex phone offices on the main square next to Restaurant Plaza Leza, 0800-2300, and on Salas between Av 10 and 15. There are also expensive **Computel** offices in town, eg at the cruise ship dock. **Telephone centre** for long distance on corner of Rafael Melgar and Calle 3 Sur. Also public telephone *caseta* at Av 5 esq Calle 2, 0800-1300, 1600-2100.

Tulum *p72*
Banks HSBC, Av Tulum open 0900-1900, has an ATM, but doesn't change TCs. **Scotiabank** further along the same road is open Mon-Fri, 0900-1600, changes TCs and cash. Several *casas de cambio* in Av Tulum closer to the **ADO** terminal.
Telephone and internet Long-distance phones on Av Tulum near and opposite the **ADO** terminal in town. Internet cafés on the same road.

Chetumal *p77, map p77*

Banks The banks all close at 1430. There are several ATMs. For exchange, **Banamex**, Obregón y Juárez, changes TCs. **Banco Mexicano**, Juárez and Cárdenas, TCs or US$ cash, quick and courteous service. Several on, or near, Av Héroes with ATMs. Banks do not change quetzales into pesos.

Embassies and consulates Guatemala, Av Héroes de Chapultepec 354, T983-832 6565. Open for visas, Mon-Fri 0900-1700. It is best to organize your visa, if required, in your home country before travel. **Belize**, Hon Consul, Lic Francisco Lechón Rosas, Rotondo Carranza 562 (behind Super San Francisco), T983-878 7728; visas can take up to 3 weeks to get, and many are only issued in Mexico City. **Internet** Eclipse, 5 de Mayo 83 between PE Calles and Zaragoza. 0930-1500, 1800-2100, not very friendly but cheap at US$3 per hr. **Los Cebollones**, Calzada Veracruz 452, T983-832 9145, also restaurant and cocktail bar. **Laundry** Lavandería Automática 'Lava facil', corner of Héroes and Confederación Nacional Campesina.

Medical services Malaria prophylaxis available from **Centro de Salud**, opposite hospital (request tablets for paludismo).

Post 16 de Septiembre y PE Calles. Mon-Fri 0800-1730, Sat 0900-1300. Packets to be sent abroad must be taken unwrapped to the bus terminal to have them checked by customs before taking them to the post office. Better to wait until another town. Parcel service not available Sat. **Western Union** office attached to post office, same hours.

Contents

Footnotes

Basic Spanish for travellers

Learning Spanish is a useful part of the preparation for a trip to Latin America and no volumes of dictionaries, phrase books or word lists will provide the same enjoyment as being able to communicate directly with the people of the country you are visiting. It is a good idea to make an effort to grasp the basics before you go. As you travel you will pick up more of the language and the more you know, the more you will benefit from your stay.

General pronunciation

Whether you have been taught the 'Castilian' pronunciation (*z* and *c* followed by *i* or *e* are pronounced as the *th* in think) or the 'American' pronunciation (they are pronounced as *s*), you will encounter little difficulty in understanding either. Regional accents and usages vary, but the basic language is essentially the same everywhere.

Vowels

a	as in English *cat*
e	as in English *best*
i	as the *ee* in English *feet*
o	as in English *shop*
u	as the *oo* in English *food*
ai	as the *i* in English *ride*
ei	as *ey* in English *they*
oi	as *oy* in English *toy*

Consonants

Most consonants can be pronounced more or less as they are in English. The exceptions are:

g	before *e* or *i* is the same as *j*
h	is always silent (except in *ch* as in *chair*)
j	as the *ch* in Scottish *loch*
ll	as the *y* in *yellow*
ñ	as the *ni* in English *onion*
rr	trilled much more than in English
x	depending on its location, pronounced *x*, *s*, *sh* or *j*

Spanish words and phrases

Greetings, courtesies

hello	*hola*	please	*por favor*
good morning	*buenos días*	thank you (very much)	*(muchas) gracias*
good afternoon/		I don't speak Spanish	*no hablo español*
evening/night	*buenas tardes/noches*	do you speak English?	*¿habla inglés?*
		I don't understand	*no comprendo*
goodbye	*adiós/chao*	please speak slowly	*hable despacio por favor*
pleased to meet you	*mucho gusto*		
see you later	*hasta luego*	I am very sorry	*lo siento mucho*
how are you?	*¿cómo está?*	what do you want?	*¿qué quiere?*
	¿cómo estás?		*¿qué quieres?*
I'm fine, thanks	*estoy muy bien, gracias*	I want	*quiero*
I'm called...	*me llamo...*	I don't want it	*no lo quiero*
what is your name?	*¿cómo se llama?*	leave me alone	*déjeme en paz/ no me moleste*
	¿cómo te llamas?		
yes/no	*sí/no*	good/bad	*bueno/malo*

Questions and requests

Have you got a room for two people?
¿Tiene una habitación para dos personas?
How do I get to_? *¿Cómo llego a_?*
How much does it cost?
¿Cuánto cuesta? ¿cuánto es?
I'd like to make a long-distance phone call
Quisiera hacer una llamada de larga distancia
Is service included? *¿Está incluido el servicio?*
Is tax included? *¿Están incluidos los impuestos?*

When does the bus leave (arrive)?
¿A qué hora sale (llega) el autobús?
When? *¿cuándo?*
Where is_? *¿dónde está_?*
Where can I buy tickets?
¿Dónde puedo comprar boletos?
Where is the nearest petrol station?
¿Dónde está la gasolinera más cercana?
Why? *¿por qué?*

Basics

bank	*el banco*	market	*el mercado*
bathroom/toilet	*el baño*	note/coin	*el billete/la moneda*
bill	*la factura/la cuenta*	police (policeman)	*la policía (el policía)*
cash	*el efectivo*	post office	*el correo*
cheap	*barato/a*	public telephone	*el teléfono público*
credit card	*la tarjeta de crédito*	supermarket	*el supermercado*
exchange house	*la casa de cambio*	ticket office	*la taquilla*
exchange rate	*el tipo de cambio*	traveller's cheques	*los cheques de viajero/los travelers*
expensive	*caro/a*		

Getting around

aeroplane	*el avión*	insured person	*el/la asegurado/a*
airport	*el aeropuerto*	to insure yourself against	*asegurarse contra*
arrival/departure	*la llegada/salida*	luggage	*el equipaje*
avenue	*la avenida*	motorway, freeway	*el autopista/la carretera*
block	*la cuadra*		
border	*la frontera*	north, south, west, east	*norte, sur, oeste (occidente), este (oriente)*
bus station	*la terminal de autobuses/camiones*		
bus	*el bus/el autobús/ el camión*	oil	*el aceite*
		to park	*estacionarse*
collective/ fixed-route taxi	*el colectivo*	passport	*el pasaporte*
		petrol/gasoline	*la gasolina*
corner	*la esquina*	puncture	*el pinchazo/ la ponchadura*
customs	*la aduana*		
first/second class	*primera/segunda clase*	street	*la calle*
left/right	*izquierda/derecha*	that way	*por allí/por allá*
ticket	*el boleto*	this way	*por aquí/por acá*
empty/full	*vacío/lleno*	tourist card/visa	*la tarjeta de turista*
highway, main road	*la carretera*	tyre	*la llanta*
immigration	*la inmigración*	unleaded	*sin plomo*
insurance	*el seguro*	to walk	*caminar/andar*

Accommodation

air conditioning	*el aire acondicionado*	power cut	*el apagón/corte*
all-inclusive	*todo incluido*	restaurant	*el restaurante*
bathroom, private	*el baño privado*	room/bedroom	*el cuarto/l*
bed, double/single	*la cama matrimonial/*		*a habitación*
	sencilla	sheets	*las sábanas*
blankets	*las cobijas/mantas*	shower	*la ducha/regadera*
to clean	*limpiar*	soap	*el jabón*
dining room	*el comedor*	toilet	*el sanitario/excusado*
guesthouse	*la casa de huéspedes*	toilet paper	*el papel higiénico*
hotel	*el hotel*	towels, clean/dirty	*las toallas limpias/*
noisy	*ruidoso*		*sucias*
pillows	*las almohadas*	water, hot/cold	*el agua caliente/fría*

Health

aspirin	*la aspirina*	diarrhoea	*la diarrea*
blood	*la sangre*	doctor	*el médico*
chemist	*la farmacia*	fever/sweat	*la fiebre/el sudor*
condoms	*los preservativos,*	pain	*el dolor*
	los condones	head	*la cabeza*
contact lenses	*los lentes de contacto*	period/	*la regla/*
contraceptives	*los anticonceptivos*	sanitary towels	*las toallas femeninas*
contraceptive pill	*la píldora anti-*	stomach	*el estómago*
	conceptiva	altitude sickness	*el soroche*

Family

family	*la familia*	boyfriend/girlfriend	*el novio/la novia*
brother/sister	*el hermano/la hermana*	friend	*el amigo/la amiga*
daughter/son	*la hija/el hijo*	married	*casado/a*
father/mother	*el padre/la madre*	single/unmarried	*soltero/a*
husband/wife	*el esposo (marido)/*		
	la esposa		

Months, days and time

January	*enero*	November	*noviembre*
February	*febrero*	December	*diciembre*
March	*marzo*		
April	*abril*	Monday	*lunes*
May	*mayo*	Tuesday	*martes*
June	*junio*	Wednesday	*miércoles*
July	*julio*	Thursday	*jueves*
August	*agosto*	Friday	*viernes*
September	*septiembre*	Saturday	*sábado*
October	*octubre*	Sunday	*domingo*

at one o'clock	*a la una*	it's six twenty	*son las seis y veinte*
at half past two	*a las dos y media*	it's five to nine	*son las nueve menos*
at a quarter to three	*a cuarto para las tres/*		*cinco*
	a las tres menos quince	in ten minutes	*en diez minutos*
it's one o'clock	*es la una*	five hours	*cinco horas*
it's seven o'clock	*son las siete*	does it take long?	*¿tarda mucho?*

Numbers

one	*uno/una*	sixteen	*dieciséis*
two	*dos*	seventeen	*diecisiete*
three	*tres*	eighteen	*dieciocho*
four	*cuatro*	nineteen	*diecinueve*
five	*cinco*	twenty	*veinte*
six	*seis*	twenty-one	*veintiuno*
seven	*siete*	thirty	*treinta*
eight	*ocho*	forty	*cuarenta*
nine	*nueve*	fifty	*cincuenta*
ten	*diez*	sixty	*sesenta*
eleven	*once*	seventy	*setenta*
twelve	*doce*	eighty	*ochenta*
thirteen	*trece*	ninety	*noventa*
fourteen	*catorce*	hundred	*cien/ciento*
fifteen	*quince*	thousand	*mil*

Food

avocado	*el aguacate*	fish	*el pescado*
baked	*al horno*	fork	*el tenedor*
bakery	*la panadería*	fried	*frito*
banana	*el plátano*	garlic	*el ajo*
beans	*los frijoles/*	goat	*el chivo*
	las habichuelas	grapefruit	*la toronja/el pomelo*
beef	*la carne de res*	grill	*la parrilla*
beef steak or pork fillet	*el bistec*	grilled/griddled	*a la plancha*
boiled rice	*el arroz blanco*	guava	*la guayaba*
bread	*el pan*	ham	*el jamón*
breakfast	*el desayuno*	hamburger	*la hamburguesa*
butter	*la mantequilla*	hot, spicy	*picante*
cake	*el pastel*	ice cream	*el helado*
chewing gum	*el chicle*	jam	*la mermelada*
chicken	*el pollo*	knife	*el cuchillo*
chilli or green pepper	*el ají/pimiento*	lime	*el limón*
clear soup, stock	*el caldo*	lobster	*la langosta*
cooked	*cocido*	lunch	*el almuerzo/la comida*
dining room	*el comedor*	meal	*la comida*
egg	*el huevo*	meat	*la carne*

minced meat	*el picadillo*	sausage	*la longaniza/el chorizo*
onion	*la cebolla*	scrambled eggs	*los huevos revueltos*
orange	*la naranja*	seafood	*los mariscos*
pepper	*el pimiento*	soup	*la sopa*
pasty, turnover	*la empanada/*	spoon	*la cuchara*
	el pastelito	squash	*la calabaza*
pork	*el cerdo*	squid	*los calamares*
potato	*la papa*	supper	*la cena*
prawns	*los camarones*	sweet	*dulce*
raw	*crudo*	to eat	*comer*
restaurant	*el restaurante*	toasted	*tostado*
salad	*la ensalada*	turkey	*el pavo*
salt	*la sal*	vegetables	*los legumbres/vegetales*
sandwich	*el bocadillo*	without meat	*sin carne*
sauce	*la salsa*	yam	*el camote*

Drink

beer	*la cerveza*	ice/without ice	*el hielo/sin hielo*
boiled	*hervido/a*	juice	*el jugo*
bottled	*en botella*	lemonade	*la limonada*
camomile tea	*la manzanilla*	milk	*la leche*
canned	*en lata*	mint	*la menta*
coffee	*el café*	rum	*el ron*
coffee, white	*el café con leche*	soft drink	*el refresco*
cold	*frío*	sugar	*el azúcar*
cup	*la taza*	tea	*el té*
drink	*la bebida*	to drink	*beber/tomar*
drunk	*borracho/a*	water	*el agua*
firewater	*el aguardiente*	water, carbonated	*el agua mineral con gas*
fruit milkshake	*el batido/licuado*	water, still mineral	*el agua mineral sin gas*
glass	*el vaso*	wine, red	*el vino tinto*
hot	*caliente*	wine, white	*el vino blanco*

Key verbs

to go	**ir**
I go	voy
you go (familiar)	vas
he, she, it goes,	
you (formal) go	va
we go	vamos
they, you (plural) go	van

to have (possess)	**tener**
I have	tengo
you (familiar) have	tienes
he, she, it,	
you (formal) have	tiene
we have	tenemos
they, you (plural) have	tienen

there is/are	hay
there isn't/aren't	no hay

to be	**ser**	**estar**
I am	soy	estoy
you are	eres	estás
he, she, it is,		
you (formal) are	es	está
we are	somos	estamos
they, you (plural) are	son	están

This section has been assembled on the basis of glossaries compiled by André de Mendonça and David Gilmour of South American Experience, London, and the Latin American Travel Advisor, No 9, March 1996

Index

Titles available in the Footprint *Focus* range

Latin America	UK RRP	US RRP
Bahia & Salvador	£7.99	$11.95
Buenos Aires & Pampas	£7.99	$11.95
Costa Rica	£8.99	$12.95
Cuzco, La Paz & Lake Titicaca	£8.99	$12.95
El Salvador	£5.99	$8.95
Guadalajara & Pacific Coast	£6.99	$9.95
Guatemala	£8.99	$12.95
Guyana, Guyane & Suriname	£5.99	$8.95
Havana	£6.99	$9.95
Honduras	£7.99	$11.95
Nicaragua	£7.99	$11.95
Paraguay	£5.99	$8.95
Quito & Galápagos Islands	£7.99	$11.95
Recife & Northeast Brazil	£7.99	$11.95
Rio de Janeiro	£8.99	$12.95
São Paulo	£5.99	$8.95
Uruguay	£6.99	$9.95
Venezuela	£8.99	$12.95
Yucatán Peninsula	£6.99	$9.95

Asia	UK RRP	US RRP
Angkor Wat	£5.99	$8.95
Bali & Lombok	£8.99	$12.95
Chennai & Tamil Nadu	£8.99	$12.95
Chiang Mai & Northern Thailand	£7.99	$11.95
Goa	£6.99	$9.95
Hanoi & Northern Vietnam	£8.99	$12.95
Ho Chi Minh City & Mekong Delta	£7.99	$11.95
Java	£7.99	$11.95
Kerala	£7.99	$11.95
Kolkata & West Bengal	£5.99	$8.95
Mumbai & Gujarat	£8.99	$12.95

Africa	UK RRP	US RRP
Beirut	£6.99	$9.95
Damascus	£5.99	$8.95
Durban & KwaZulu Natal	£8.99	$12.95
Fès & Northern Morocco	£8.99	$12
Jerusalem	£8.99	$12
Johannesburg & Kruger National Park	£7.99	$11
Kenya's beaches	£8.99	$12
Kilimanjaro & Northern Tanzania	£8.99	$12
Zanzibar & Pemba	£7.99	$11

Europe	UK RRP	US RRP
Bilbao & Basque Region	£6.99	$9.9
Granada & Sierra Nevada	£6.99	$9.95
Málaga	£5.99	$8.95
Orkney & Shetland Islands	£5.99	$8.95
Skye & Outer Hebrides	£6.99	$9.95

North America	UK RRP	US RRP
Vancouver & Rockies	£8.99	$12.95

Australasia	UK RRP	US RRP
Brisbane & Queensland	£8.99	$12.95
Perth	£7.99	$11.95

For the latest books, e-books and smart phone app releases, and a wealth of travel information, visit us at:
www.footprinttravelguides.com.

footprinttravelguides.com

Join us on facebook for the latest travel news, product releases, offers and amazing competitions: www.facebook.com/footprintbooks.com.